A Journey of Faith

Lord, we beseech thee mercifully to receive the prayers of thy people, which call upon thee; and grant that they may both perceive and know what things they ought to do, and also have grace an power faithfully to fulfille the same, through Jesus Christ our Lord. Amen.

Scottish Book of Common Prayer
1637

A Journey of Faith

The Story of Dardenne Presbyterian Church
1819–2004

Diane C. Rodrique

iUniverse, Inc.
New York   Lincoln   Shanghai

A Journey of Faith
The Story of Dardenne Presbyterian Church 1819–2004

iUniverse, Inc.

For information address:
iUniverse, Inc.
2021 Pine Lake Road, Suite 100
Lincoln, NE 68512
www.iuniverse.com

ISBN: 0-595-32638-2

Printed in the United States of America

Contents

Acknowledgements

Many thanks to William Humberg, Hu Weikart, Ray Baer, Evan Totten, Harold and Dorothy Morgan, Jim Mouser and Diane Smith for their invaluable assistance

Preface

The author and historian, Thomas Cahill, once said that most people view history as a series of catastrophes. He went on to say that, interspersed in these events are benevolent moments we know as moments of grace. They are the times when man extends a helping hand, risks his life for another or in some way acts in a manner that is above and beyond the call of duty. They are the times when those who have a personal relationship with Jesus Christ can see His love at work. These moments of grace can be seen throughout the history of Dardenne Presbyterian Church.

There are numerous events during our 185-year history when the Lord called upon His faithful to continue His work despite the circumstances. During these times we have faced, as a church and as individuals, many hardships. Yet, despite epidemics, fires, floods and even scandals, we have persevered. Interspersed in these events are moments of grace that can only be described as miracles. Strengthened by miracles and encouraged by those who came before us, we have continued our journey of faith along the path and have known much joy in doing so.

It is this path of joy that leads us to focus our efforts on mission work. This follows a long-held Presbyterian tradition. The first Presbyterian minister to the St. Louis area was Rev. Albert Salmon Giddings, a missionary. Our church was founded by a missionary, Rev. Charles S. Robinson. It is only appropriate that we continue to serve God in that capacity and proceed with the work begun so many years ago. While some may think our Mission Conferences and our local and worldwide mission efforts to be our ultimate achievement, we see it as simply another remarkable opportunity to serve and glorify our God. In the coming years may we continue to walk this path of love, following the footprints of devotion left by those who came before us, and may we continue to serve our Lord with joyous hearts.

It is with love and gratitude that this book is dedicated to the founders of our church, whose love of God and faith in Him established Dardenne Creek Presbyterian Church:

Rev. Charles S. Robinson, John and Jane Naylor, James Naylor,
Adam and Jessie Zumwalt, Mrs. Elizabeth McPheeters, and
Nathaniel and Mary Tucker

Diane C. Rodrique
July 2004

Chapter 1

Of Pioneers and Missionaries

Overview: The First Miracle

When all facts are considered, it is a miracle our church was ever founded. Prior to the early 1800's there were several factors responsible. The confusion caused by lack of communication, precarious travel conditions and political rivalry before, during and after the colonization of the Louisiana Territory reads like a comedy of errors. Because of intense rivalry between, England, Spain and France, the three major European powers at the time, communications were hampered. Restricted by several centuries of "family feuds" among the royal houses, violence, wars, and squabbles over real estate and even social superstitions, it is a wonder that peace treaties could be secured at all. Often, peace was claimed only by another marriage among the aristocracy or an exchange of real estate, such as the Louisiana Territory.

Travel was precarious and subject to the whims of weather. Travel agents did not exist and the few luxury accommodations available were reserved for the aristocracy. On land, paved roads did not exist, although some brick streets were found in major cities. Coaches and wagons were little more than horse-drawn wooden boxes. Sailing ships weren't much better. During the late 1700's and early 1800's, a ship could transport passengers from western England to Nova Scotia in about thirty days. Shipping from other locales could take up to nine or ten weeks. A trip from France to the Louisiana Territory was not only expensive but could easily take close to a year and be extremely dangerous. Journeys of any length became even more difficult once a traveler left the more "civilized" towns back east. For an overland journey, a horse and rider could cover twenty miles in one day—in good weather. Travel by coach or wagon could take even longer. Roads were practically nonexistent especially the further west one traveled on the new continent. Bridges did not exist over the Mississippi.

Enter Church and State

The Vatican provided a confusing note to the situation, as well. When Christopher Columbus returned from the New World he brought riches and news of wealth and abundant land. King Ferdinand and Queen Isabella of Spain petitioned Pope Alexander VI to declare that Spain owned all land west of the Azores. By the time Spain had established a colony in Cuba, other European nations, specifically England and France had sent explorers to the New World in hopes of discovering riches to fill the ever-dwindling royal coffers. At times, each group ignored the territorial claims of other countries in order to gain a foothold. Spain, of course, held to the Papal edicts of 1493 that declared all lands belonged to Spain. England, having broken with the Church of Rome during the reign of Henry VIII, felt no compunction to honor Spanish claims or the Vatican declarations. Often, within months or years, England or France would claim the same territory acknowledged by the Vatican as belonging to Spain.

As the English colonies formed on the East coast of the continent, the Spanish claimed and settled most of the southern and western part of the continent. France, a predominantly Catholic nation also, chose to honor the Vatican claims on occasion, when it suited their needs. However, French explorers concentrated on the northern and midwestern portions of the North American continent. Despite any Vatican declarations, both France and England blatantly claimed large portions of land by "right of priority in discovery." By 1607, both countries ignored Spanish claims and Vatican declarations as the English established Jamestown on the Eastern coast and the French established Quebec.[1]

As the seventeenth century progressed, all three countries continued to claim land despite any prior "right of discovery." One such claim was in 1682, by the

---

1   Encyclopedia of History of St. Louis, (St. Louis, MO. 1899) p. 583.

French explorer Robert Cavalier, Sieur de La Salle, who claimed a vast area in the Missouri and Mississippi River valleys which later became just a small portion of the Louisiana Territory. In his claiming, he formally declared all the country that drained by the great river, from the Alleghenies to the Rocky Mountains to be the property of the King of France.[2] Unfortunately, Charles I of England had given a large portion of the same land in a royal grant, to Sir Robert Heath. Still another part of it belonged to Spain by Vatican declaration and "right of discovery."

Another factor was that "state of the art" communications at the time consisted of parchment, quill and ink, and any trusted courier with a good horse. Communication, or rather, a lack of communication between the European powers played a major role in the confusion as to which country owned what area. Another problem stemmed from treaties between the countries. Several years could elapse from the time a treaty was signed, the news reached the territory and a new commander arrived in the area. Again, the Louisiana Territory is a prime example of the problem.

Because of its location and size, the Louisiana Territory became an excellent negotiating piece for several decades, especially between France and Spain. The gem in this choice piece of real estate was New Orleans located at the mouth of the Mississippi and thus accessible to shipping the newfound riches of the territory to Europe. Additionally, New Orleans and small towns dotted throughout the territory provided supplementary revenue through taxes.

The first settlers in what would become the Missouri Territory arrived a few years after La Salle claimed the area as a French possession. The first white settlers were a group of Jesuit missionaries, who established the Mission of St. Francis Xavier, around 1700, near the present St. Louis.[3]

In 1765, Pierre Laclede moved northward from New Orleans to establish the fur-trading post of St. Louis on the Mississippi River. Louis Blanchette moved south from Canada to an area on the Missouri River within forty miles of Laclede's St. Louis site. However, Blanchette did not stay. Instead, he returned to Canada until 1769 when he returned with a group of settlers. However, during his absence, the Treaty of Paris had transferred ownership of the land from France to Spain. Due to slow communication and travel, Laclede, and Blanchette didn't realize they had established French settlements in Spanish territory. In fact, before Blanchette could return with his followers, the town of St. Louis had been named the French capital of the Louisiana Territory in 1765.[4] By the time word reached

---

2   Ibid., p. 583.
3   E. Couch, *Missouri Trivia*, Rutledge Hill Press, (Nashville, TN. 1992), p. 75.
4   Ibid., p. 9.

St. Louis that it was the capital of the area, the town and the surrounding territory was officially Spanish territory—courtesy of yet another treaty in November of 1763 between the two powers. However, Spain did not claim the land until 1764 and the first Commandant didn't even arrive in St. Louis until 1770.[5]

As the ink dried on new treaties and power changed hands, any settlers in the area had to make necessary adjustments. Some towns were renamed to suit the "new management" When the Louisiana Territory changed from French to Spanish control, the French settlement of Les Petite Côtes became known as San Carlos del Misury.[6] With the Treaty of Ildefonso of 1800, the Louisiana Territory was owned by the French for such a brief period that the name remained as San Carlos until 1804, when the United States claimed ownership and anglicized it to St. Charles.[7]

"That Presbyterian Revolution"

While Spain and France played Monopoly with the Louisiana Territory, England turned her sights to India and Africa. Both continents were ripe for "colonization" and exploitation of its citizenry and natural resources. However, by 1776, the colonies of America had England's full attention again as a growing trend toward independence took shape. The concept of colonial independence from England grew at an alarming rate. Thomas Payne's controversial booklet, *Common Sense* fueled the fire. In a letter to her husband, John, a future First Lady of the United States, Abigail Adams wrote, "This flame is kindled and like lightening it catches from soul to soul."[8]

The concept that a country could survive without a monarch and be, "conceived in liberty and dedicated to the proposition that all men are created equal." was unthinkable. Yet, it was in the making. And it was the Presbyterians' fault—at least according to those close to King George III. The purpose behind demanding independence began to emerge, in 1764, when Britain began to establish a series of taxes, which many colonists felt were outrageous. With heavy taxation and no representation in Parliament, colonial leaders felt they had the right to establish their own political and economic system independent of the mother country. With an estimated 250,000 Scots/Irish in the colonies, most well-educated and Presbyterian, it is understandable why many in England felt the rising unrest was

5   Ibid., p. 584
6   Couch, Ernie, *Missouri Trivia*, (Rutledge Hall Press, Nashville, TN. 1992), p. 22
7   Couch, Ernie, *Missouri Trivia*, (Rutledge Hall Press, Nashville, TN. 1992), p. 27
8   Comminger, H. S. and Morris, R. B., *The Spirit of Seventy-Six*, (De Capo Press, New York 1975) p. 1

a "Presbyterian problem." One wag in Parliament referred to the rebellion as, "that Presbyterian revolution" and an editorial cartoon in a daily London newspaper showed "Cousin America running away with a Presbyterian Parson." There was some truth to these statements. Since the beginning, the Church of Scotland/Presbyterian Church had developed the reputation of social and political involvement in the community.

By 1776, when the Declaration of Independence was signed, the Presbyterian Church had a strong representation. Among the signers of that document, twelve were Presbyterians, including the only minister to sign it, John Witherspoon. A direct descendant of John Knox, (the founder of the Church of Scotland) Witherspoon was President of Princeton University and Seminary.

Rev. Witherspoon encouraged his students to become involved in the social and political issues of the time. In fact, his views on colonial independence were so well known that the British General William Gage referred to Princeton students as "seeds of sedition." It was a phrase he would later use to indicate all who had the audacity to rebel against His Majesty, George III. Either Gage was intuitive or he had an excellent spy system in place within the colonies. After the war, a significant number of former Princeton students openly admitted to membership in the Samuel Adams rebel group known as The Sons of Liberty. By 1783, "that Presbyterian revolution" had created a new country conceived in liberty and the Preamble to its Constitution included the phrase, "…one nation under God."

Not all are created equal

With the surrender of British General Charles Cornwallis at Yorktown, Virginia, the war came to a close and former colonists now citizens of the United States, began to exercise their new-found freedoms. While there were many reasons for the westward trek, most families made the arduous journey because the land was plentiful and the soil was rich. Continuous farming in the original thirteen colonies had depleted the nutrients in the soil and most farmers could no longer support their families A majority of the farmers and settlers from the East Coast of America began the westward journey to the Kentucky, Tennessee and Ohio territories. Eventually the slow westward expansion brought farmers across the Mississippi River to the Spanish Territory. The primary rule of any Spanish-held area was that it was Catholic territory. The majority of the settlers were of various Protestant denominations with a significant portion being Presbyterian or Methodist.

Although the colonists fought for their right to pursue, "…life, liberty and the pursuit of happiness." the settlers who moved westward found other laws in effect in the Louisiana Territory and often those depended entirely on who held the land—The French or the Spanish. Land ownership was determined by a variation of an archaic law enacted during the reign of the French monarch, King Louis XIII, in 1615. Known collectively as The Code Noir Laws, the edicts were designed as an effort to control minority populations, originally the minority Jewish population in France. The laws began to apply to any group of people or individuals who were not French or Catholic. In the case of the Louisiana Territory, the prevailing logic said that French laws would apply in a French territory, especially those that could control the ever-increasing African slave population, and Protestants. Eventually as the Spanish took over the territory, they in turn adopted the same law that conveniently allowed the ruling minority to control the general populace.[9] However the Spanish were willing to make exceptions to the rule. In the late 1700's Daniel Boone, a Quaker, gathered a small group of Scots/Irish farmers from the Carolinas, Virginia and Tennessee and moved into the Upper Louisiana territory of the Femme Osage Valley with some hefty incentive from the Spanish government.

Despite the fact that new settlers brought religious diversification, a variation of the Code Noir Laws remained in effect because the Territory was held by the Spanish, and they were aligned with the Church of Rome. As a result, a man could wake up a Presbyterian, be baptized a Catholic by lunchtime and own land by sundown—and still be a Presbyterian in his heart. Despite the law, most settlers and new landowners held to their religious beliefs. In Spanish-held territory there was no difference between church and state as there was in the newly formed United States.

However, the famous explorer and pioneer, Daniel Boone, was an exception to this "Catholic only" rule. The Spanish had openly courted Boone, with full knowledge that he was a Quaker. He readily accepted the Spanish proposal of several thousand acres of rich land, farm implements, and farm animals, Boone gathered his followers and began the westward trek. By July of 1800, Boone had been appointed Syndic (judge) of the Femme Osage district.[10]

The families that journeyed with Boone banded together for a variety of reasons. For many, it was the opportunity to settle in an area where the soil wasn't depleted as it was "Back East" after several hundred years of use. Additionally, in a sparsely populated area there was more land available to a man in the new territory. Most settlers hoped for nothing more than a piece of good land and plenty of space where a man could grow enough food to feed his family and lead a peaceful life following the turmoil of the American Revolution. Crossing the Missouri River, Boone and

9   George Washington Cable website/Historical context-2003-p.1.
10   Bloom, Jo Tice, *Gateway Heritage Magazine* (Missouri Historical Society, St. Louis, MO. 1985) p.37.

his group settled in the prairie area between Dutzow and Dardenne Prairie, in the Femme Osage Valley.

It's probable that many of the Scots/Irish pioneers in Boone's party were related to or had known of a brave soul who had given his life at Culloden. This was the bloody battle that, coupled with hundreds of years of British oppression, brought about the demise of political strength within the Scottish Clan system. Afterwards, some families fled Scotland. Other families were separated and sent, courtesy of the British government, to Ireland and the colonies where they were to blend in to the culture and become "proper British citizens." Many who were sent to the colonies did so as bondservants and spent many years in servitude before they gained their freedom. Some families who came with Boone, perhaps their fathers, or the settlers themselves, had fought the British during the American Revolution. Now, as citizens of the newly formed United States of America, they were free to live their lives without fear of being driven from their lands, threatened by the King's soldiers or living in poverty from heavy taxation. Most importantly, they could worship God without fear of retaliation.

Boone's followers understood the hardships of pioneer life and they knew the wilderness offered few comforts. They understood the risks and the back-breaking labor involved in the daily struggle for survival in frontier life. However, they were also aware that, with hard work and God's guidance, the new life offered not only more land, but more freedom and more opportunity. The hardships of their way of life merely strengthened their faith in God, and they were resolved to give their families a brighter future.

As word spread of Boone's arrival to the Territory, and the Spanish offered vast land grants, others followed and the area began to thrive. Some new arrivals were rather enterprising. By 1797, Capt. James Piggott, for instance, began a ferry service across the Mississippi at St. Louis and charged $2 for a horse and rider.[11]

The Louisiana Purchase

Boone and his group had settled in the Femme Osage Valley only a few years when, Spain ceded all of the Louisiana Territory back to France. By then, France realized it was quickly losing any real claim to the continent and bargained with the prime piece of real estate. Except for the Canadian provinces, the French had little to show from their efforts in the New World. France needed revenue more than the real estate and the sparsely settled territory couldn't begin to raise enough tax money or meet the financial demands of the French government as

---

11   Couch, Ernie, *Missouri Trivia* (Rutledge Hill Press, Nashville, TN. 1992) p.101.

the province of Quebec had done. Additionally, Napoleon knew he couldn't raise an army to defend the area, let alone finance and transport soldiers to the Louisiana Territory. Even then, settlers from the newly created and ever-expanding United States had begun to arrive. By the early 1800's the French dictator planned to become the Emperor of Europe—but first he would have to conquer Europe, and that could be costly. However, Napoleon had a source of ready cash to finance his dream. He sold the Louisiana Territory to the United States. When the final papers were signed, Napoleon had relinquished all rights to the Louisiana Territory for $15 million dollars. With 828,000 square miles in the area, it averaged out to about 3-4 cents per acre.[12] Although the vast area in the Louisiana Purchase was rich in natural resources and conducive to settlements it would be another year before the United States physically claimed the region.

Few settlements of any size existed in the territory. St. Charles had been founded a little over 30 years before. St. Louis, founded in 1765 and just a few years older, was a small town of approximately 900 people with fewer than 200 log buildings. Further downstream on the Mississippi River was the largest town in the entire Upper Louisiana Territory. With a population of almost one thousand residents, Ste. Genevieve had served as a home base for Pierre Laclede and Auguste Chouteau when they sought to establish a fur trading post known as St. Louis.

In 1804, when the Corps of Discovery arrived, St. Charles was only a small French village with a few log cabins struggling to survive on the Missouri River. Due to limited travel and communication, the Spanish Commandant Delassus refused to allow Meriwether Lewis and his Corps of Discovery to cross over from the Illinois side of the Mississippi to begin their westward journey as ordered by President Thomas Jefferson. Commandant Carlos Delassus had not been informed that the Territory had been relinquished to France, and in turn, sold to the United States. As a result, it was a curious ceremony that relinquished Spanish command of the territory on March 9, 1804. Delassus resigned his authority to Captain Stoddard, Lieutenant Worral and Captain Meriwether Lewis of the United States. The Spanish flag was lowered, the French flag raised for twenty four hours, then lowered as the United States flag was raised to full staff and remained. Within one day, the citizens of the Louisiana Territory had lived under the rule of three different countries. As the American flag was raised, the area was officially recognized as part of the United States.

Captain Lewis had been the driving force for the final ceremony. In the previous year, as a long-time friend and personal secretary to President Thomas

12   Ibid., p. 90.

Jefferson, he had been asked to organize an exploratory party along the upper portion of the newly acquired land and report his findings.

Jefferson allocated $2,500 for the trip. In his June 19, 1803 letter to his friend, William Clark, Lewis asked, "…If there is anything…which would induce you to participate with me in it's fatiegues, [sic] it's dangers and it's honors, believe me there is no man on earth with whom I should feel equal pleasure in sharing them as with yourself."[13] Lewis began the trip on the Ohio River from Pittsburgh on August 31, 1803.

Clark replied to Lewis's letter, "I will chearfully [sic] join you and partake of the dangers, difficulties and fatigues."[14] He then joined Lewis' party at Louisville on October 15th. Along the way they stopped at Army outposts and gathered more men for the trip. Yet, It would be more than two years before the explorers returned with accounts of rich land and abundant wildlife, two of the most important items needed for new settlements. Jackson Dykman, historian for Time Magazine, notes that the party gathered supplies at St. Louis, then wintered from December to May 13, 1804 at Camp River DuBois on the Illinois side of the Missouri River. Fortified for the expedition that would change the face of America, the Lewis and Clark Expedition began its westward trek from St. Charles, Missouri on May 20, 1804.[15] The Corps of Discovery consisted of two leaders, Lewis and Clark, plus about forty men, a teenager named Sacagawea, her husband, a French-Canadian trader and trapper and York, a slave to William Clark.

They traveled by boat, horse and on foot for two years, four months and ten days and completed the mission with only one fatality.[16] A phenomenal record when one considers there were no advanced medical assistance available, no wonder drugs, and only rudimentary herbal concoctions.

Although the Indians were fascinated with York, they were more interested in what the Corps had with them to trade—especially the shiny medallions showing a likeness of President Thomas Jefferson on one side and a symbolic handclasp on the other.[17] At one point, Clark even traded his coat for assistance from one tribe.

Unfortunately, there was a downside to this historic event. First, Jefferson was disappointed in the results. His primary objective had been to find a water route to the Pacific Ocean. He had also hoped for easily accessible land and abundant wildlife with a good water supply for settlers. The peace agreement with the

13   Jones, Landon Y. Time Magazine, *Leading Men*, (Time, Inc. New York 2002) p. 54.
14   Ibid., p.56.
15   Lancaster, David. Where Magazine, *Lewis & Clark in St. Louis*, (St. Louis, MO. 2002) p.10.
16   Ibid., p. 18.
17   Kirn, Walter. Time Magazine, *Lewis & Clark Bicentennial*. (Time, Inc., New York, 2002) p.40.

Indians became an idealistic dream. As a result, the first edition of the journals didn't even appear until eight years after the completion of the expedition.

Perhaps the saddest tale to come of this adventure was that of Captain Meriwether Lewis. A chronic depressive, he ended his life in 1809 in a Tennessee inn on his way to Washington, D.C. The entire purpose of the trip was to defend his expedition expenses to a bureaucrat in the War Department.[18]

Clark remained in Missouri where he became the Indian Agent for the Missouri Territory. Nearly a decade later, on October 1, 1812, he was appointed by Congress as the first Governor of the newly organized Territory of Missouri. It was during this time that Clark and his wife, Julia, took in Sacajewea's children to raise and educate. During the expedition William Clark had grown fond of little Jean Baptiste, born during the Corps of Discovery's expedition. Jean Baptiste and his younger sister, Lizette, being raised by Clark, broaches the subject of what became of Sacajewea. Shoshone legend claims she lived to be 100 years old. However, in all probability, she died at an early age, as Clark suggests in a letter to a friend in 1820.

When Clark died in 1838 he was buried on the farm owned by his nephew, Col. John O'Fallon. Later, when Bellefontaine Cemetery was established, his body was moved to that cemetery. In October 1904, his monument was unveiled during the World's Fair.[19]

St. Louis: A wild, and lawless town

By 1808, the Territory was flourishing. Publisher, Joseph Charless began publication of the Missouri Gazette which was published in both French and English,[20] and the first book in the area, The Laws of the Territory of Louisiana had been published.[21] St. Louis was still considered to be far from civilization, and much of the region was unsettled. The rough and rugged riverfront village was seen as nothing more than a crude, lawless and uncivilized town with a few log cabins and mud streets.

Yet, approximately forty miles northwest of St. Louis was an entirely different and quieter lifestyle. Dardenne Prairie was still an area of unfenced land and crude dirt trails. Few creeks had bridges, and what few bridges did exist were usually washed out with the first spring floods. Herds of livestock roamed at will. The land was good for farming and although bears and wolves still populated the area, wildlife was plentiful. During good weather, it could take as much as half a day to reach St. Charles by horseback, and even longer by wagon. In the dry

---

18   Ibid., p.41.
19   A Tour of Bellefontaine Cemetery., (St. Louis, MO. undated) p. 3.
20   Crouch, Ernie. *Missouri Trivia*, (Rutledge Hall Press, Nashville, TN, 1992) p.130.
21   Ibid., p. 115

weather of summer, great clouds of dust would form as travelers moved along the roads. During the spring and autumn, the same dusty trails could become a sea of mud during rainy weather. Winter brought ice and snow. Most travel depended largely on the weather and the season.

The weather and poor travel conditions weren't the only problems that plagued settlers. Residents of the area were stunned by the loss of Captain James Callaway and his St. Charles Company Rangers during the Indian uprising of 1815. Most of the region had been spared such attacks due to defensive measures taken by Callaway, Daniel Boone and his sons, Daniel Morgan and his youngest son, Nathan.

The men had organized the reinforcement of stone and log forts throughout the area that had been built about ten years earlier. With safety in mind, the settlers who arrived in the area between the late 1700's and early 1800's built several forts as protection against the Indians. Prior to 1812, when it seemed evident that the United States would once again go to war with Britain, Boone and the settlers reinforced the forts. Although seldom used, they provided peace of mind and a haven of safety. Boone's Fort was located in the Darst's Bottom, and Howell's Fort was on Howell Prairie. Pond Fort on Boone's Lick Trail was the home of Robert Baldridge and his son, Malachai. Several sources list Malachai as one of the first victims killed and scalped by Indians before the Indian uprising in 1815.[22]

White's Fort was on Dog Prairie, Kountz' Fort, not far from Nicholas Kountz' tavern, was on Boone's Lick Trail, Zumwalt's Fort in present-day O'Fallon and Castlio's Fort near Howell Prairie. Others were located near Troy, Marthasville and Wright City. Unfortunately, in 1815, as Callaway and his Rangers patrolled the area outside Washington, Missouri near Loutre Creek, they were attacked by Indians. As a result, Callaway and his Rangers met death because they had ventured outside the safety areas of the forts they had helped reinforce. Later that year, representatives from nineteen different tribes gathered at the old Spanish fort at Portage des Sioux to sign peace treaties with U.S. Commissioners.[23]

The settlers knew they were responsible for their own welfare and could not rely on the U.S. Government for assistance. Even at the beginning of the War of 1812, there were fewer than 200 federal troops stationed in the whole of the Missouri territory.[24]

Despite the dangers and hardships, the settlers prevailed and flourished in the new territory. Some stayed as others continued westward. From this auspicious

---

22 George, Alan Wentzville Journal, *Forts Once Dotted County Landscape.* (Suburban Journals, St. Louis, MO. Oct. 10, 2001) p. B1.
23 Crouch, Ernie. *Missouri Trivia*, (Rutledge Hall Press, Nashville, TN. 1992.) p. 22.
24 Ibid., p. 94.

beginning, the Missouri Territory became known as a launching area for westward travel and exploration. Wagon trains formed in St. Louis, St. Charles, Joplin and St. Joseph, the Missouri Territory became known as the Mother of the West and St. Louis, the Gateway to the West. As a result of these journeys that began in the Missouri Territory came the Santa Fe Trail, The Salt Lick Trail and the Oregon Trail.

Until that time, it was said that the Boone's Lick Trail was "as far west as a man could go." An account from St. Charles on April 23, 1819 said that from the prior October more than 271 wagons had traveled out for "Boone's Lick Country." While the most common means of local travel was by horse or farm wagon, "mover wagons" or "prairie schooners" were seen on the Trail as more people headed west to settle the new territory. While horses were used for local wagons, the journey west required a sturdier animal. For most schooners, the choice was either mules or oxen. Few realize the expense involved with the journey west. The wagon itself, supplies for several months and the oxen could cost hundreds of dollars. A good team of oxen, could cost as much as $200. The amount needed for a trip west could be considered a tidy sum even by today's standards.

It was sheer determination on the part of Mr. Stephen Hempstead that would change the untamed town of St. Louis. Mr. Hempstead, originally from Connecticut, was best known as a Revolutionary War hero who had served with Nathan Hale. Years later Hempstead would become an Elder in the Bonhomme Presbyterian Church and would soon prove himself to be something of an "Elder" to the community. Upon his arrival to the area, Hempstead took one look at the city of St. Louis and began a long and persistent correspondence with the Connecticut Mission and Bible Society. St. Louis, he felt, was in dire need of spiritual guidance.

On March 31, 1811, Hempstead noted in his diary, "I occasionally attend Mass at the Catholic church and discuss religion with the itinerant Methodist and Baptist preachers, but sorely miss the discourses of the classically educated clergy of the Presbyterian and Congregational churches."[25]

Finally, after several years, his numerous requests for missionaries to the Missouri Territory were answered. In late 1815, word arrived that a missionary would supply the area in the spring of the following year. Hempstead's letter writing campaign proved to be instrumental in establishing the Presbyterian Church in the Missouri Territory. His support for the church would remain steadfast through the coming years. From the first Presbytery meeting in St. Louis in 1817, Hempstead was listed in attendance and continued to serve the Presbytery well into

25   Giddings-Lovejoy Presbytery, St. Louis. Missouri Giddings-Lovejoy Board Records 1817-1834

the late 1820's.[26] Hempstead would leave his mark on the St. Louis area. Eventually, most of the original acreage of his farm became Bellefontaine Cemetery.

As the Missionary Society had promised, the first missionary arrived the next spring. A graduate of Williams College and Andover Seminary (Harvard), Rev. Albert Salmon Giddings was ordained in December of 1814 and spent the following year riding circuit in Massachusetts. In his second year of ordination, Rev. Giddings, was appointed by the Bible Society to "attend the spiritual guidance of those most in need" and was promptly sent to the wild and lawless town of St. Louis.

His arrival in the city on April 6, 1816 coincided with an article which appeared in the Missouri Gazette that

Rev. Albert Salmon Giddings
Photo courtesy of Giddings-Lovejoy Presbytery,
St. Louis, Missouri

same day. The editorial was headlined as "CAUTION!" and the accompanying story went on to warn St. Louis citizens against the supposed perils of eastern missionaries. Some would think it was not a fortuitous beginning, however, speculation holds the article was encouraged by those who had an interest in the lucrative gambling and saloon businesses. The article was merely further proof that Rev. Giddings services were definitely needed in the lawless town.[27]

26 Giddings-Lovejoy Presbytery, St. Louis. Missouri Giddings-Lovejoy Board Records 1817-1834
27 Dardenne Presbyterian Church Archives. *175th Anniversary Celebration.* (O'Fallon, MO. 1995) p.5

More missionaries are called

Within months of his arrival, Rev. Giddings sought to establish a church in the Bonhomme Bottoms area (Chesterfield). But, with a busy planting season in progress he decided to return to the area at a later date. He then moved on to the Bellevue Settlement. On August 2nd of 1816, the Bellevue Church of the Bellevue Settlement (now known as Concord Presbyterian Church in Caledonia, Missouri) was established. Concord has the distinction of being the first Presbyterian church west of the Mississippi River. Caledonia also holds another significant first. On December 1, 1807, still named the Bellevue Settlement, thirty settlers from the area gathered for the first Presbyterian sunrise service west of the Mississippi River.

Rev. Giddings returned to the Bonhomme area and by November of 1816 formed the Bonhomme Presbyterian Church. Once it was established, he turned his attention to the city of St. Louis. There, on November 23, 1817, the First Presbyterian Church of St. Louis was founded. Within eighteen months of his arrival, Rev. Giddings had organized three churches in the Missouri Territory. Presbytery records show that by then, fortunately, more missionaries had arrived in the area. Revs. Thomas Donnell, and John Matthews provided the additional support Rev. Giddings required.

Included in the group that was received by the Presbytery on October 4, 1817 was Rev. Timothy Flint. Records indicate Flint had arrived in St. Louis within weeks of Giddings arrival, the previous year. However, Flint instead sought to establish a school which eventually failed. Little wonder when one considers his impressions of the St. Louis citizenry. "My reception was cold. The Americans of influence are generally Tennesseans and Kentuckians sufficiently disposed to cherish prejudice against eastern people." He described the area as being without religion: "It is a common proverb of the people, that when we cross the Mississippi, 'we travel beyond the Sabbath.'"[28]

By August 1818, Flint had been elected Moderator of the Missouri Presbytery but by the following spring would choose to leave. On April 29, 1819, he requested his leave of the Presbytery and permission was granted. He was, in addition to his pastoral duties, a writer and editor and was already considered a popular author back East. Rev. Flint was not fond of prairie life and oddly enough, despite his dislike, romanticized it. He did remain in the area until about 1822, probably to gather information on Daniel Boone.

It's probable having lived and traveled in the St. Charles County area, that Flint met Boone on more than one occasion. Flint wrote one of the first biographies on the pioneer frontiersman. While much has been written about Daniel Boone, it

---

28   Stadler, Frances Hurd. *St. Louis Day by Day*. (Patrice Press, St. Louis, MO. 1990) p. 89.

was Flint who first embellished Boone's image with superhuman accomplishments such as killing a bear with a hunting knife. Curiously, having experienced the hardships of prairie life, Flint chose to romanticize the stories of Boone. In doing so, Rev. Flint is responsible for many of the other legends that add to Boone's colorful personality.

This exaggeration of heroes became an acceptable literary style immediately after the American Revolution when Parson Gentry Weems wrote tall tales about such heroes as George Washington and Paul Revere. It became a practice that continued for well over one hundred years. Heroes from George Washington to Buffalo Bill Cody would have their accomplishments liberally embellished for the dramatic effect and the reader's entertainment.

Although Rev. Flint's services were no longer available, God had provided two more dedicated workers. At the same April 29th Presbytery meeting that granted Rev. Flint's request, Rev. Charles S. Robinson and another missionary, Rev. David Tenney presented their credentials and were accepted[29] It was at this meeting that the Presbytery deemed it expedient to form a Missionary society. Giddings. Robinson and Tenney were chosen to prepare a Constitution and report the next day. On April 30th, the Presbytery accepted the constitution and the American Home Missionary Society of Missouri was formed.[30] Robinson was not only one of the founders but the first to be employed by the group and sent to St. Charles.

---

29 Courtesy: Giddings-Lovejoy Presbytery, (St. Louis, MO. 1995.) *Minutes of the Presbytery of* St. Louis pp. 401-402.

30 Courtesy: Giddings-Lovejoy Presbytery. *Minutes of Missouri Presbytery.* April 29-30, 1819. S. Giddings, clerk. p. 4

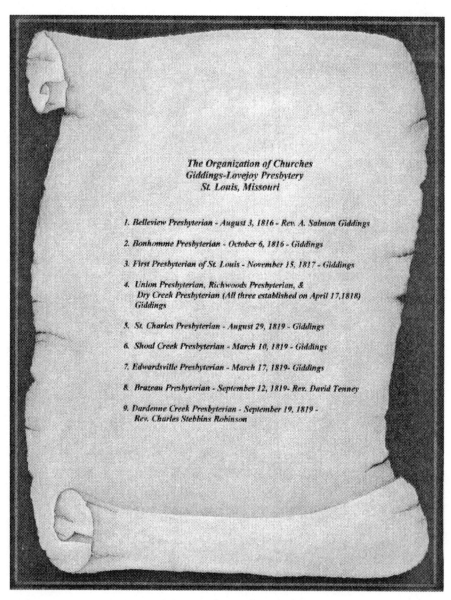

Organization of churches in Giddings-Lovejoy Presbytery.

Chapter 2

The Flame Is Kindled

According to the Presbytery minutes of that same April meeting, "The Rev. Charles Robinson is required to supply at St. Charles and its neighborhood." The 25-year-old Robinson was assigned to the St. Charles church. His duties, as prescribed by the Presbytery, consisted of providing service part-time to the church and then riding circuit in St. Charles County. Although primarily in St. Charles, his work extended over a large part of the central part of Missouri Territory. He was the only Presbyterian missionary for nearly all the region north of the Missouri River.[31]

Those who came to know Robinson said he was "…of good ability, with fine literary accomplishments, earnest and a devoted minister." Tradition holds that Rev. Robinson well understood self-denial. Once, when he was out of food and money, he found a silver dollar imbedded in the earth. It sufficed for his family until another source of money came through. In later years as his family grew, he supplemented his income by teaching. Riding circuit in St. Charles County, Rev. Robinson's ministerial area included, Dardenne Prairie, and the Boone's Lick Trail.[32]

---

31 Courtesy of the Giddings-Lovejoy Presbytery. *Minutes of the Presbytery of St. Louis,* St. Louis, MO. p. 402.
32 Dardenne Presbyterian Church Archives. *175th Anniversary.* Dardenne Prairie, MO.

Meanwhile, David Tenney, a former Andover Seminary classmate of Rev. Robinson's, had presented his credentials to the Presbytery at the same time as Robinson. Charged by the Londonderry Presbytery "to serve the destitute parts of our country," Rev. David Tenney was sent to St. Louis. On September 12th of 1819, he formed the Brazeau Presbyterian Church at Brazeau, Missouri. He immediately returned to the St. Charles area to assist Rev. Robinson at the St. Charles church while the latter moved to form the church at Dardenne Prairie. However, Tenney's time would be limited in the Missouri Territory. Only a few weeks later, on September 27th, he became ill and passed away on October 12th, one month to the day after founding the Brazeau church. He was only 34 years old when he died and had been ordained less than two years.[33]

Joining forces

As Tenney was forming the Brazeau church, Rev. Charles Robinson met with store owner John Naylor and a group of his neighbors to establish yet another church for the area that would be known as Dardenne Creek Presbyterian Church. (To commemorate the event, the State of Missouri and the Daughters of the American Revolution placed a marker on the north side of Highway N, just one mile west of the current Dardenne Presbyterian Church.)

Naylor, who had been an Elder in the Presbyterian Church in Washington, Kentucky, owned the store located just off the Boone's Lick Trail. The store was a hub of activity for the pioneer community. Friends and neighbors gathered to purchase everything from flour and salt to nails and tools.

When time permitted, they discussed events of the day, especially when a copy of the *St. Louis Inquirer*, *The Missouri Gazette* or the *Missouri Argus*, arrived at the little prairie store.

There was much news to be discussed at the time. James Monroe had just been inaugurated as the fifth President of the United States and William Clark, Governor of the Territory, announced the disappointing news that Missouri's petition for statehood had been denied.

A few miles southeast of the Naylor place was Nelson's Mill, used primarily for cutting lumber but also for grinding corn. To the northeast was a mill that ground buckwheat and corn. Very few businesses were found along the trail. Other than the general store or an occasional tavern, the only other business was salt manufacturing started by Nathan Boone and Daniel Morgan Boone. Most pioneer families were self-sufficient, and needed few outside services. However,

---

33 Brazeau Presbyterian Church, *175th Anniversary Booklet*. p. 2.

the predominately Scots/Irish settlers did not have a church and Rev. Robinson sought to rectify that situation.

With David Tenney's return from Brazeau, Rev. Robinson arranged a meeting on September 18,1819 with Naylor and neighbors who were committed to establishing a Presbyterian church in the Dardenne area. Reverend Robinson met with John Naylor, his wife Jane (nee Coulter) and their son, James, Mrs. Elizabeth (nee Coulter) McPheeters, Adam Zumwalt and his wife, and Nathaniel Tucker and his wife. Although Tenney is credited in some sources as assisting Robinson with establishing Dardenne, he isn't listed in the minutes of the meeting. As a result, his role, as noted in outside sources is vague. However, since Tenney was now in the St. Charles area it's likely he played some role. Due to the fact that this was about the time he became ill, it's possible his role was seriously limited or curtailed by the illness that would claim his life.

According to church records, the first meeting began with a prayer and the group set about determining the basics for forming their church. Presbytery records from the next meeting indicate that John Naylor was chosen Ruling Elder. There was no worship service held that first day. It should be noted that Nathaniel Tucker, the clerk for the first meeting, listed the date as September 18th. When Rev. Robinson filed the date with the Presbytery he listed the date as September 19th.

Later, as services were held, either at the store or in one of the homes of a founding member, others from the community began to attend. Through the years, the church membership would read like a "Who's Who of St. Charles County." To this day, the names of early Dardenne church family members are still well known throughout the county: Boone, Howell, Castlio, Zumwalt, McCluer, Watson, Boyd, Currier, Macheny, MacIlveny, Stewart, Callaway and Bates. The majority began attending worship services before the first church, a log cabin, was built by Dardenne Creek.

Within a few months, the original nine members had grown to a twenty—member congregation. Adults and children met at the Zumwalt's home in a full day of prayer, fellowship and meals. During the winter months, church was seldom held, but when travel was possible, the members would arrive at the Zumwalts' on Saturday night.

The Minutes of the Presbytery of St. Louis, page 403, make note of a letter Rev. Robinson wrote to the Home Missionary Society concerning the Dardenne church. "At the Dardenne, the prospects are generally brightening. I have preached there during the summer, one-half the time. Last month the sacrament of the Lord's Supper was administered. It was an interesting season. Five who were heads of families were admitted to the church on profession of faith, three of whom were baptized. Some of them were from a family that resided in this State years before it was ceded to the American Government...A few years since this whole connection knew not the Sabbath but to profane it; now they are, I trust, singing the song of redeeming love. And what a change the gospel has wrought in that family in the small settlement of Dardenne."

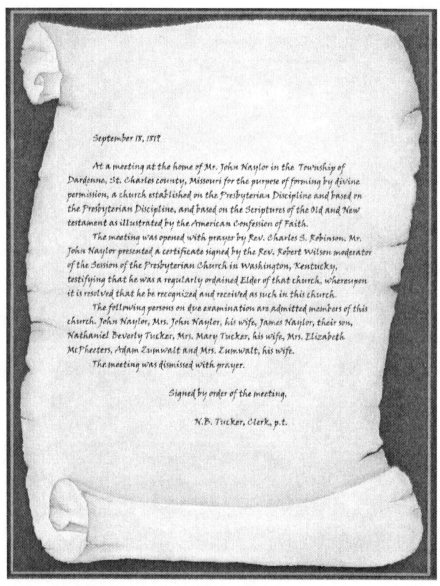

September 18, 1819

At a meeting at the home of Mr. John Naylor in the Township of Dardenne, St. Charles county, Missouri for the purpose of forming by divine permission, a church established on the Presbyterian Discipline and based on the Presbyterian Discipline, and based on the Scriptures of the Old and New testament as illustrated by the American Confession of Faith.

The meeting was opened with prayer by Rev. Charles S. Robinson. Mr. John Naylor presented a certificate signed by the Rev. Robert Wilson moderator of the Session of the Presbyterian Church in Washington, Kentucky, testifying that he was a regularly ordained Elder of that church, whereupon it is resolved that he be recognized and received as such in this church.

The following persons on due examination are admitted members of this church. John Naylor, Mrs. John Naylor, his wife, James Naylor, their son, Nathaniel Beverly Tucker, Mrs. Mary Tucker, his wife, Mrs. Elizabeth McPheeters, Adam Zumwalt and Mrs. Zumwalt, his wife.

The meeting was dismissed with prayer.

Signed by order of the meeting,

N.B. Tucker, Clerk, p.t.

Minutes of the First Meeting of the Dardenne Presbyterian Church, Establishing the Church and Admitting Its First Members

Missouri becomes a state

The area thrived as more families began to settle the Missouri Territory. By now, a weekly stagecoach run had begun from St. Charles all the way to the town of Franklin. Although denied admission once, Missouri entered the Union as the twenty-fourth state. However, due to political pressure by Southern representatives in Congress, it was allowed to do so as a slave state. (Maine had entered the Union the previous year as a free state) Southern representatives sought to insure an equal balance in representation by bringing Maine in as a free state and Missouri as a slave state. St. Charles was chosen as the state capital for the twenty-fourth state of the Union and William Clark, of the Lewis and Clark Expedition, was appointed Governor. Although the first session of the Missouri General Assembly met in the Missouri Hotel in St. Louis,[34] the first "state capitol" offices were located above the Peck Bros. General Store on Main Street in St. Charles. The Missouri government met there until 1825[35]. Regardless of political doings in the nation's capital, the settlers continued to pour into the area and settle while others moved westward in a continuing expansion of the United States.

Seemingly untouched by the event at the time, but concerned about the disturbing slavery issue, Dardenne residents continued with their daily lives. Only years later did they realize how Missouri entering the Union as a slave state would prove to have dire consequences for the Dardenne church.

At the Dardenne

It was also during this time that Dardenne Creek Presbyterian began expanding. Within four years of its formation, and through the generosity of Adam and Margaret Zumwalt, the church was given five acres of land. Originally part of a Spanish land grant to Zumwalt, the property is now part of the current Busch Wildlife Area. The deed to the church called for "5 acres being part of the tract of land conveyed and conceded by the Spanish government to the said Adam Zumwalt." The deed went on to state that the church was "to have and to hold the said lot or parcel of land to the use of said, John Taylor, Andrew Zumwalt, Thomas D. Stephenson and James Baldridge trustees aforesaid and their successors as aforesaid in trust to hold the same for the purpose of maintaining a church for public worship, according to the Presbyterian forms and discipline."[36] Signing

34 Stadler, Frances Hurd. *St. Louis Day by Day* (The Patrice Press, St. Louis, MO. 1995) p. 178
35 Ibid., p. 178.
36 Barbee, Kent. *Correspondence with Hubert Weikart*, Chairman History Task Force, Dardenne Presbyterian Church. August 25, 2001.

the deed at that time was Theophilus McPheeters, a stepson of Mrs. Elizabeth McPheeters, one of the founding members. He was also a Justice of the Peace and a member of the church. For reasons unknown, the deed was not recorded until many years later in 1838. By then, McPheeters had been involved in a church scandal, issued a letter of apology to the Dardenne congregation and moved his family to Vicksburg, MS., where he became a wealthy planter.

Although seldom mentioned in most texts on the church history, Elizabeth A. Watson's book, *Heritage and Promise* notes that the deed mentioned five acres and a log church. Apparently the church was built prior to the land being deeded to the church. However, in 2002 that information was confirmed with the presentation of the original deed to the church. For some reason, the deed was left in care of the Stevenson family who had been quite active in the church for many years. Through the years, most seemed to forget about the deed and some assumed it was lost forever. Yet, in November of 2002, the original 1823 deed was returned to the church through the generosity of historian, Kent Barbee. Although faded and torn, and crumbling on the corners, the original deed yielded a little known fact about the generous Dardenne benefactors, the Zumwalts.

Instead of signing their names, they made their mark, which was witnessed by others. Even though neither of the Zumwalts could read or write, they were instrumental in settling St. Charles County, and generously provided assistance to Dardenne Presbyterian. Prior to aiding Dardenne, they had offered a portion of their land for one of the reinforced log forts that dotted the area. It was known as Fort Zumwalt and the name is easily recognized in St. Charles County today. Even the local school district carries the name of Zumwalt.

Despite floods, drought, and prairie fires, the church at Dardenne Creek flourished. With land and a log church, there was now space for a cemetery. Tradition holds that several plots were included within its boundaries that were set aside for settlers who died while moving west.

Changes and controversy within the church

Two of the first changes to come to Dardenne were the deaths of the two men who had led the way for Presbyterian churches in the Missouri Territory. In February of 1828, Rev. Salmon Giddings passed away. After being moved several times, his grave is now located at Bonhomme Presbyterian Church Cemetery. Marked with a simple gravestone, designed by Baxter Watson, the pioneer missionary is remembered with the words, "Well done good and faithful servant." The back of the tombstone lists the twelve churches established by an extraordinary man.[37]

---

37   Watson, Baxter. Carved in Stone Tour, Bonhomme Presbyterian Church Cemetery. May 13, 2003.

Charles Robinson had established a home in St. Charles where, in March of 1821, he married the former Ms. Jane Becket, a member of the St. Charles church. The officiating minister was well known to Robinson, his bride and the St. Charles congregation. As the first minister of the St. Charles Presbyterian Church, Rev. Timothy Flint returned to perform the ceremony for his friends. Robinson, who suffered from poor health, died of tuberculosis just seven years after he had married Ms. Becket. He was buried in the Lindsey family plot in Elm Pointe cemetery in St. Charles.[38] Jane Becket-Robinson passed away in 1834 and was buried beside her husband. Her sister, Margaret, had married Mr. Thomas Lindsey before arriving in St. Charles. Originally from Scotland, Lindsey was a prominent businessman and the first Elder in the St. Charles Presbyterian Church. Although tradition holds that the Robinsons had seven children, there is no mention of their fates after the death of their parents except for the two boys who were sent back to the Becket family in South Carolina. On September 25, 1828, the day after the tenth anniversary of his ordination, Robinson passed away.

The Presbytery steps in

It was April 1830 when serious and damaging allegations began to arise among members of Dardenne. The ensuing scandal caused a division among the congregation that would last many years. Finally, their arguments were presented to the Presbytery for a decision. By April 5th when the Presbytery met, the accusations had become so harsh, the Presbytery resolved to hold hearings on the charges. Those accused included the current Stated Supply pastor, Rev. William Lacy, John Naylor, and his son James Naylor, both founding members of the church. Additionally, charges were brought against, Theophilus McPheeters, stepson of a founding member and John Gill. Normally, Presbytery meetings were held in St. Louis or St. Charles, but beginning on April 19,1830, they met for seven days at Dardenne Creek Presbyterian Church. At that time, the seven-member board resolved to sit as a judicial court to try the cases on the agenda.

First on the program were charges against Mr. John Gill, an Elder of the church. Although, meeting records do not indicate the exact charge against him, they were serious enough that upon hearing them read, he supposedly pled guilty and "professed repentance." Two Elders were designated to meet and pray with Mr. Gill, then report back to the committee the following day.

There were several issues surrounding Dardenne's then current Stated Supply Pastor, Rev. William S. Lacy. First, there was a move within the church to have

---

38 Courtesy: Giddings-Lovejoy Presbytery. *Minutes of the Presbytery of St. Louis.* p. 405.

Lacy ousted. This was led by Rev. John Ball who just happened to be a member of the Presbytery board. His efforts not only included a verbal campaign, but a petition signed by seven members of the twenty-six member church. Second, Lacy was accused of playing a flute and providing dance music for young ladies and gentlemen. Eventually, Lacy was retained as Stated Supply but the charge of playing music was seen by the board as "unchristian conduct." Upon Rev. Lacy's repentance, the matter was considered closed.

The trials of John Naylor, James Naylor and Theophilus McPheeters had an entirely different outcome.

Mr. McPheeters was first on the list. After much testimony and two witnesses later, the Board voted McPheeters as being "guilty of insubordination and willful contempt of court" for refusing to answer questions and leaving the court during session. Two days later, he was found guilty of the charges and "suspended from communion with the church until a time when he is thoroughly repentant." It's interesting to note that although McPheeters was a member of Dardenne, Rev. Lacy, then stated supply of that church, declined to vote on the matter. The charge? According to McPheeters family files, Mr. McPheeters, a Justice of the Peace, was charged with inciting a riot in St. Charles over the return of some slaves.

For some time prior to the meeting, there had been accusations and gossip tossed between the Naylors, McPheeters, Lacy and Ball. When Naylor's daughter married Judge Tucker's son, there had been a promise of a gift of slaves to the newlyweds from Judge Tucker. At one point, a year after the wedding, Naylor had written to Tucker about the slaves. The letter was presented as evidence at the hearing because of one particular line. The line that somebody had tried to erase. Somebody, who to this day is unknown, tried to remove a reference to one of Judge Tucker's slaves. In the letter, Tucker had replied to Naylor's request with, "I cannot accept your proposition for the slave, Sukey."

Although nothing explicit is mentioned in the meeting minutes, apparently whatever Naylor proposed was enough to condemn him in the eyes of the Presbytery. After a two-day trial, Naylor and his son, James, were suspended from the Sacraments of the Church.[39]

When the Presbytery convened a few months later in October 1830, the board was informed that both the Naylors and McPheeters had appealed to the Synod. The Synod upheld the Presbytery's decision and their appeal was denied. It would be ten years before Naylor would be reconciled with the Dardenne congregation.[40] It would be 1860 before his son, James returned.

39 Courtesy of the Giddings-Lovejoy Presbytery. *Minutes of the Missouri Presbytery. April 1830.* pp. 39-49.
40 Ibid., p. 49.

Not so for Theophilus McPheeters. In July of 1832, McPheeters issued a letter to the Presbytery and the members of Dardenne church. His apologetic letter assured all concerned that he was truly repentant. Although he returned to Dardenne, shortly afterward, in 1834, he moved his family to Vicksburg, Mississippi. McPheeters and his family then removed to Natchez, Mississippi where they remained. He apparently succeeded because the 1850 U.S. Census listed Theophilus McPheeters as a planter with a net worth of six thousand dollars, which was considered a sizable fortune at the time.[41]

Nor was John Naylor idle during his time away from Dardenne. According to several meeting notes, he was quite active and in a decision-making capacity as an Elder in the St. Charles Presbyterian Church. In 1844, Naylor returned to Dardenne, and only then because of a division in the Presbyterian Church. According to Dardenne membership records, his son James did not return to the church for thirty years and was not restored to membership until October 26, 1860.

With the passing of Giddings and Robinson, the 1830's brought significant transformations for the churches and congregations in the area, particularly the Dardenne congregation. After the turmoil of the scandal of 1830, Rev. William S. Lacy supplied the Dardenne pulpit and led a congregation that included, twenty-six members, five Elders and a total of forty attendees in the new Sabbath School. Much of this came about as a result of Mr. Lewis Howell and Dr. Robert McCluer. Howell, an educator, had begun using the "creek church" as a schoolhouse during the week when weather permitted. During this time he learned of a new concept in Christian education known as Sabbath School. The first Sabbath School Union had formed in England in the late 1700's and by the 1830's had become popular with many churches in both England and the United States. As an educator, Christian and Presbyterian, Howell found the Sunday School concept appealing.

With financial assistance from Elder Dr. Robert McCluer, a Sunday School Charter was established for Dardenne church through an organization known as the Interdenominational Sabbath School Union. In 1830, Mr. Lewis Howell paid an agent of the Missouri and Illinois Sabbath School Union two dollars for the Charter. The first Sunday School classes at Dardenne began with a total of $4 in books. At first, the Sabbath School Union seemed to be a combination Sunday School and lending library. The classes became popular and continued regularly through the 1920's. Suspended for some forty years until the 1960's, the Sunday School classes began to meet in the Rock Church; some classes were even held outdoors. Sunday School classes are now available for all ages. Every Sunday morning, preschoolers, school age children, teens and adults gather for a Sunday

41 McPheeters, Harold L., The McPheeters Family History, *Theophilus McPheeters* (Atlanta, GA. 1996) p. 1.

School class. Although a significant amount of money at the time, the six dollars spent by Mr. Howell and Dr. McCluer for the charter proved to be a sound investment.

As the church settled into a peaceful existence and wounds began to heal, a new challenge faced the church and the community. In 1834, tragedy struck in many areas, including St. Charles County. In 1834, '49 and '66, cholera epidemics swept through the area claiming many lives. In the 1834 epidemic, the lives of one prominent church member and his son were lost. Elder, and financial contributor to the Sunday School Charter, Dr. Robert McCluer passed away first. His nine-year-old son, Mo, succumbed to the deadly disease twenty-four days later. McCluer served as an Elder at Dardenne for four years prior to his death. Afterwards, his widow and children, moved to St. Charles briefly, but would return to Dardenne Prairie a decade later. Dr. McCluer's daughter, Nannie McCluer, would prove to play a significant role in the little country church.

Chapter 3

A House Divided

By now, the sparsely populated area of Dardenne Prairie had begun to grow considerably. With the coming of the railroad, there was a significant increase in the St. Charles County residents. Between 1830 and 1840, the population mushroomed from 4,320 to more than 7,000 people. With this expansion came the demand for more riverboat, stagecoach and railroad services to and from the prairie to the city. Demand was high for any form of transportation that could keep pace with appeals for additional goods and services required to meet the needs of the ever-increasing population

Nationally, the slavery issue was drawing increased attention. By now, Walker's Appeal a pamphlet that was stirring the slavery issue had been read, circulated and re-read throughout the East. Written by David Walker, the anti-slavery booklet, was praised by those who favored abolition and vilified by those who justified slavery.[42] It was about this time that the Anti-Slavery Society of Boston had formed in response to the Southampton insurrection the year before.[43] In

---

42   Grun, Bernard. *The Timetables of History* (Simon and Schuster, New York, NY. 1991) p. 392.
43   Ibid., p. 397.

that incident, Nat Turner had led slaves in a revolt that killed fifty-five white men.[44] Both sides used that incident to their advantage. Abolitionists felt it would not have happened if the men had been free men. Those in favor of slavery blamed the abolitionists for encouraging the attack.

While the slavery issue continued to divide families and friends, an equally emotional issue was beginning to develop in St. Louis. Since the early 1830's the Presbytery had begun to assess the schools in the region. By 1838, Presbyterians, Unitarians, and Catholics had drawn battle lines over the issue of teaching the Bible in school. In April 13, 1838, *The Republic* reported the results of one such meeting. Mr. Henry B. Miller, an attendee, noted that, "The question was warmly debated, there was considerable excitement, the question was not so fully adhered to as it should have been. Unfortunate sectarian prejudices and party malignity were too strongly shown on this occasion…the Catholics were mostly against the measure; the Protestants were divided, but I think the majority were in favor…" After much debate, Mr. Miller noted, a vote was taken for an indefinite postponement which was carried.[45] The author doesn't mention if the issue was ever resolved. It probably was tabled indefinitely. This was an auspicious beginning, since the city had only two public schools and both had opened only 11 days before.[46]

The Civil War's first martyr

Rev. Elijah P. Lovejoy had arrived in the St. Louis area in 1827 and taught school for several years before he became editor of the St. Louis Times. During that time, he was a member of the St. Louis Debating Club that had been formed in 1828. The exclusive membership of the Society read like a Who's Who of St. Louis Achievement.[47]

It was during this time, 1827-1828, that Lovejoy attended revival services led by Rev. Albert Salmon Giddings at the First Presbyterian Church in St. Louis. It was a result of those services that Lovejoy eventually decided to enter Princeton Theological Seminary. He completed the three-year course in thirteen months and was ordained in 1833. With encouragement from local businessmen, he returned to the St. Louis area to edit a religious newspaper, *The St. Louis Observer*.[48] Additionally, he was a pastor for Des Peres Presbyterian and stayed with that

---

44 Ibid., p. 394.
45 Stadler, Frances Hurd, *St. Louis Day by Day* (The Patrice Press, St. Louis, MO. 1989) p. 69.
46 Ibid., p. 62.
47 Ibid., pp. 116-117.
48 College Avenue Presbyterian Church,150th Anniversary, *Elijah Parish Lovejoy* (Alton, IL. 1987) p. 6.

church until he was forced out of the St Louis area. He then moved his family to St. Charles.

From the beginning, his outspoken editorials on slavery in the St. Louis Observer began to draw fire from the opposition. Eventually, Lovejoy was driven out of both St. Louis and St. Charles because of his fiery stand on the slavery issue. Immediately following a particularly fiery abolitionist sermon preached at St. Charles Presbyterian, Lovejoy and his family was forced to flee to Illinois.

As a free state, Illinois became a safe haven for abolitionists. Lovejoy moved his newspaper to Alton, and renamed it *The Alton Observer.* Even after the move, his candid abolitionist editorials continued and

The Rev. Elijah P. Lovejoy
Image courtesy of the Giddings-Lovejoy
Presbytery St. Louis, Missouri

pro-slavery resistance was fervent in what was considered a safe area. "A loaded musket is standing at my bedside, while my two brothers, in an adjoining room, have three others, together with pistols, cartridges, etc. And this is the way we live in the city of Alton!"[49] This was written about a month before he was murdered.

In January 1837, Rev. Lovejoy was installed as the first pastor of the Upper Alton Presbyterian Church (now College Avenue Presbyterian) but served the congregation only ten months. Lovejoy had moved his newspaper to Alton in the summer of 1836 and continued his crusade against slavery. Printing presses were repeatedly destroyed. When new presses were ordered and delivered by steamboat, they were taken under cover of darkness to a warehouse. News of the arrival spread and mobs stormed the warehouse that was defended by Lovejoy and a few friends. When the roof was set on fire, Lovejoy came out of the warehouse to fight the fire and was killed.[50] He was buried on November 9, 1837 on what

---

49 Poindexter, Mark. St. Charles County Heritage, Vol 21, No. 1—January 2003 *A Right Smart* Little Town. An Anecdotal History of St. Charles, Part VI. (St. Charles, MO. 2003) p. 9.
50 Stadler, Frances Hurd, *St. Louis Day by Day.* (The Patrice Press, St. Louis, MO. 1989) p. 212.

would have been his thirty-fifth birthday.[51] Rev. Lovejoy has come to be known as the "first martyr of the Civil War." As this drama played out in Alton, another was beginning to take shape in the state capital of Springfield. No one realized at the time that an assemblyman elected to the legislature would one day lead the nation as it fought over the slavery issue. Presbyterian Abraham Lincoln had been elected to the Illinois General Assembly in 1834. However, he preferred his quiet law practice and time with his family and friends. Yet, it was the same family and friends that encouraged him to run for the legislature and would continue to encourage him until he was elected to the Presidency in November of 1860.

Old School, New School

Nationally, within the Presbyterian Church, an ever-widening division was occurring over the slavery issue. Abolitionists of the industrial Northeast claimed owning slaves was immoral. Slaveholders, mostly of the agricultural South, claimed it was an economic issue. However, abolitionists, slaves and slaveholders all claimed membership in the Presbyterian Church. While the slavery issue fueled the split within the church, other differences, allowed to exist and grow, existed in how the basic Presbyterian doctrine and governing beliefs were presented to new members—especially by the missionary preachers. The disagreement had begun decades before when Congregationalists and Presbyterians joined forces to provide missionary efforts to the new territories that were opening up. By the 1830's many felt that the missionaries and the mission churches were not teaching traditional Presbyterian doctrine. The split would prove to be just as divisive to the church as the Civil War was to the nation. In Philadelphia, 1837, after debate and controversy, four Synods were excluded from the Presbyterian Church. Those who adhered to the Presbyterian doctrine became known as the "Old School." The opposition was known as "The New School" or the "Constitution Presbyterian Churches in the United States."

While the Dardenne church voted to remain with the "Old School," the St. Charles congregation was divided on the issue. The St. Charles Presbyterian Church faced a dilemma. Part of the church adhered to the "Old School" and became known as the Main Street Church, located on South Main Street in St. Charles. Those who followed the "New School" beliefs established the Constitution Presbyterian Church on North Main Street. That group was led by Rev. James Gallaher. Eventually, in 1866, the church on South Main would disband, but members from Main Street Church moved to Dardenne.

---

51 College Avenue Presbyterian Church, 150th Anniversary, *Elijah Parish Lovejoy*, (Alton, MO. 1987) p. 7.

In November of 1844, several members of the Main Street Church were received into the Dardenne congregation on Certificate of Transfer. Some of those received were members of the Preston, Castlio, McCluer, Woodson and Howell families. A familiar name was returned to the Dardenne rolls that day, Mr. John Naylor, one of Dardenne's founding members and the first Elder of the church had come home. Despite continued growth in the region, until 1841, the Dardenne church was still the only Presbyterian church in the country area of St. Charles. Most members lived in what is now the Defiance area and traveled a considerable distance to attend services. In November 1841 a new Presbyterian church, Femme Osage, was organized approximately two miles from the Nathan Boone home on the farm once owned by Flanders Callaway. A decade later the few Femme Osage members that remained would merge with the Dardenne church when theirs could no longer continue.

It was just about this time that the USS Creole incident created a stir between the pro-slavery supporters and abolitionists. A ship carrying slaves from Virginia to Louisiana was commandeered by the slaves who then sailed it to Nassau where they remained as free men.[52] The incident fueled more impassioned arguments on both sides of the issue. Yet, the coming years would prove the Nassau event to be just another incident involving slavery. In fact, it would seem rather mild compared to the violence that would soon erupt and engulf an entire nation.

Called and Installed:
Rev. Thomas Watson

In 1844 Dardenne celebrated its twenty-fifth anniversary and claimed seventy-nine members and five elders. Until then the pastors who served Dardenne were Stated Supply provided by the Presbytery. In October of that year, however, Dardenne's Session called Rev. Thomas Watson to be the church's first installed pastor.

Graduating from Princeton Seminary in 1844, Watson was licensed to preach by the Presbytery of St. Louis. Although he was a licentiate minister to the Dardenne congregation for five months prior, it was not until October 1844, that the Session voted to call

Rev. Thomas Watson
First Installed Pastor of Dardenne
Presbyterian Church 1844–1888

---

52 Grun, Bernard, The Timetables of History. (Simon and Schuster, New York, 1991) p. 408.

Rev. Watson as the installed minister. In November of that year, he accepted the call and was installed at Dardenne Creek Presbyterian. Rev. Watson was not a stranger to the area. Having arrived with his family in 1837, Watson had originally planned to follow his father in the newspaper business. However, the chance invitation by Dr. William Potts of the Second Presbyterian Church of St. Louis changed his plans. Joining Dr. Potts on his rounds to St. Charles and Dardenne, Thomas Watson realized his calling was to the church, not a newspaper.[53]

The year following the arrival of Rev. Watson, the Dardenne Creek Presbyterian Church acquired another two acres of land for the sum of one dollar. The area deeded by John Nelson and his wife was located directly north of the land donated by Andrew Zumwalt and his wife. The Nelsons were Episcopalians but attended Dardenne because there was no church of their denomination in the area. Between 1845 and 1850 the Nelsons issued three deeds which included two pieces of land and usage rights to the Dardenne Creek Springs for one thousand years.[54]

In the mid-1840's a brick church was built to accommodate the growing congregation. Although little is known about the physical structure of the church, most churches in the area were built similar to the Newport Presbyterian Church in Potosi, MO. That building measures about thirty by fifty feet with three support columns located in the center of the room. High-backed wooden benches provided seating for the congregation with the men sitting on one side of the church and the women and children occupying the other side. Slaves sat in the balcony.

Because travel was so difficult, church attendance became a day-long affair. During this time, two services were held on Communion Sundays, one in the morning and one in the afternoon.

A preparation service was held, usually at the morning service or the evening prior to the Communion Service. At that time, each communicant received a small lead pellet as a sign they were in good standing with the church. As they approached the Lord's Table for communion, the lead pellet was given to an Elder. For services, many families arrived by wagon, carriage or horseback the night before and camped out in their wagons or some makeshift shelter. Picnic-style family dinners were normal practice. Large baskets of food, packed in anticipation of the event, were set out on separate tables scattered about the woods around the church.

The formation of the St. Charles West Plank Road in 1849 was supposed to ease travel difficulties. Large wooden planks were laid end to end along the trail but within a short time, the planks began to warp and rot. Within a year, the

53 Dardenne History Task Force, Dardenne Presbyterian Church Archives. *175th Anniversary Celebration.* (Dardenne Prairie, MO. 1994) pp. 16–17.
54 Ibid., p.16.

planks had been removed to use as firewood.[55] It seems as though Missouri has always had problems with her roads. A law passed in 1822, stated that all males ages 16-45 were required to assist in the upkeep of the local roads in their districts.[56] That would have included the first East-West thoroughfare (as such), the Boone's Lick Trail. The St. Charles West Plank Road was not the only road system to fail during that era. All seventeen of the Plank Roads throughout the area were eventually used as firewood.

Services were not always solemn events. The St. Louis Post Dispatch printed one such story that had almost been lost to time. It seems, one Sunday, in the Brick Church, a portion of one of the center-support columns broke and fell to the floor, very close to the pulpit. Rev. Watson ignored it and continued his sermon. Minutes later, a large scorpion crawled from beneath the shattered wood and skittered across the floor to the women's side of the church. In attendance that Sunday was a Captain Charles Woodson, who quickly executed the little intruder with his cane. Here was proof that perhaps not all of God's creatures were welcome. Despite the sideshow, Rev. Watson continued with his sermon.[57]

During the time that the cities increased in size and the plains decreased, telegraph service had been established between St. Louis and "back East" and the last of the wild buffaloes had been seen in Missouri.[58] It was also a time of literary greatness. Herman Melville, Nathaniel Hawthorne, Ralph Waldo Emerson, and Henry David Thoreau were joined by a new writer whose work added to the growing conflict of abolitionism versus slavery—Harriet Beecher Stowe. When her work, *Uncle Tom's Cabin*, was released in 1852, it became an immediate success—at least among the abolitionists—and fanned the flames of the slavery issue. Tradition holds that upon meeting Mrs. Stowe, then-President Lincoln replied: "So this is the lady that started the war."

---

55 Boones Lick Road.
   Note that over two centuries various spellings have included: Boone's Lick, Boones Lick and Boonslick, all referring to the same subject. Different spellings found in this book are as encountered in reference documents.
56 Couch, Ernie, (compilation) *Missouri Trivia* (Rutledge Hall Press, Nashville, TN. 1992) p. 96.
57 St. Louis Post Dispatch (edition, page and date unknown)
58 Couch, Ernie, (compilation) *Missouri Trivia,* (Rutledge Hall Press, Nashville, TN. 1992) pp. 76, 164.

Chapter 4

Trial By Fire: The Second Miracle

The Struggle Begins

By 1861 most churches, including the Presbyterian, were divided on the emotional issue of slavery. By now Lincoln had been inaugurated as President and South Carolina had seceded from the Union. Prior to the country erupting in Civil War, the "Old School" Presbyterians had voted to support what they termed the "Natural Government" of Washington D.C. Further dividing the church, in December of that year, commissioners met in Augusta, Georgia at the First Presbyterian Church to form the Presbyterian Church in the Confederate States of America. It would be 1983 before the Presbyterian churches would reunite.

Officially, the Dardenne records do not indicate the political stance of its members on the slavery issue. However, the 1852 State Census showed a "free man of color" living in the home of Rev. Thomas Watson. Presbytery records show that part of the 1830 controversy in our church had been over slave ownership. Slaves were supposed to have been given as a wedding gift to the newlyweds when Elder John Naylor's daughter married church member Nathaniel Tucker's son. Additionally, a slave named Lucy was listed in the membership rolls and belonged to the Howell family. Yet the Howell family—another member of the Dardenne congregation—was shown to be one of the top five slaveholder families in St. Charles County.[59]

By January of 1861, the slavery issue was no longer just a topic of conversation; it had begun to consume the nation. The Washington Peace Convention tried to preserve the Union but the Congress of Montgomery formed the Confederacy. Fort Sumter was taken by Confederate forces and by April 12th, the country was at war. Lincoln called out the militia to suppress Confederate troops but they were victorious at Bull Run.[60]

Throughout the Territory, opinions on slavery were closely divided. Most Missourians were slaveholders, originally from the Southern states, and supported the cause. Others who were Irish and German settlers supported the Union cause. The Hon. Claiborne Jackson, Governor of Missouri at the time, was a Confederate sympathizer. The successful Unionist battle waged against a secessionist governor in a slave state all began in January of 1861 when Jackson was inaugurated as Governor of Missouri.[61] He lost no time in calling a state convention to consider the relationship between Missouri and the Union. The purpose of the gathering was to "adopt measures for vindicating the sovereignty of the State and the protection of its institutions as shall appear to them to be demanded."[62] St. Louisans counteracted the secessionist scheme of the new governor. In a Union meeting at the Old Courthouse, it was resolved that "we are not prepared to abandon the Union while any hope of adjustment remains."[63]

That is not to say that Governor Jackson and the Confederates were not without support in St. Louis. Battle lines were being drawn especially among those who held any power within the governmental structure. Gen. Daniel M. Frost wrote to Jackson late in January and informed him that the depository in St. Louis was well-armed, the commander of the depository was a secessionist and there was enough munitions to arm Confederate troops in the whole of Missouri.[64] Even Judge Alfred W. Morrison, after ten years in office, resigned as State Treasurer, rather than swear allegiance to the Union.[65]

---

59 Buschmeyer, Mary Ethel, Webbink, Eunice, Haeussermnn, Geerling, Carol, Geerling, Linn, Geerling, Greg compilation *1852 State Census, St. Charles County Missouri.* (Lineage Press, Bridgeton, MO. 1985.) pp. 1, 21.

60 Grun, Bernard. *The Timetables of History.* (Simon and Schuster, New York, NY. 1991) p. 424.

61 Stadler, Frances Hurd. *St. Louis Day by Day.* (The Patrice Press, St. Louis, MO. 1990) p. 3.

62 Ibid., p. 3.

63 Ibid., p. 4.

64 Ibid., p. 17.

65 Couch, Ernie, (compilation) *Missouri Trivia*, (Rutledge Hall Press, Nashville, TN. 1992) p. 85

Jackson ordered the board of police commissioners (men who had previously been selected by Jackson) to enforce stringent regulations regarding public gatherings in hopes of stalling any Union plots.[66] In late April of 1861 he wrote to a supporter: "I do not think Missouri should secede today or tomorrow…my judgment is that North Carolina, Tennessee and Arkansas will all be out in a few days and when they go, Missouri and Kentucky must follow. Let us then prepare to make our exit."[67]

By mid-June, before he could lead Missouri into the Confederacy, Jackson was forcibly removed from office and fled to Arkansas. Confederates were so confident that Jackson would deliver Missouri to their cause that tradition holds that one of the stars on the Confederate flag represented the state of Missouri.[68]

The first Missouri battle of the Civil War occurred on June 17, 1861, just south of Boonville. Some of the first volunteers, southern sympathizers, were from St. Charles County. The Missouri Guard, as they were called, conducted drill exercises near the St. Charles County Courthouse. The Confederate company was sworn in by Colonel Benjamin Emmons with Richard Overall as Captain and David Schultz as First Lieutenant. Men were sent to Jefferson City to obtain cannon from the State Armory, but before their arrival, the ordnance of the state had been distributed and there was none left for the St. Charles company. Without ordnance, the company was quickly forced out of the area by Federal troops from St. Louis.[69]

A German contingent under the leadership of Judge Arnold Krekel, organized a "Home Guard" and established a federal camp at Cottleville. They remained there for some time engaged in drilling and doing home guard duty. During the Civil War, only Virginia and Tennessee listed more battles within their states, with Missouri following as a close third[70]. While the Battle of Wilson's Creek, just outside Springfield, was considered the most significant, it was the battle of Westport, just south of the current Kansas City, Missouri, on October 23, 1864, that became known as "The Gettysburg of the West."[71]

---

66   Stadler, Franes Hurd. *St. Louis Day by Day*. (The Patrice Press, St. Louis, MO. 1990) p. 68

67   Ibid., p. 78.

68   Meyer, Linda. The Wentzville Journal, *The Civil War Revisted*. Vol. 40, No. 44-June 2, 2002. (Suburban Journals Publications, St. Louis, MO. 2002) p. Front page.

69   Dardenne Presbyterian Church Archives, *175th Anniversary Celebration-Civil War*. (Dardenne Presbyterian Church, Dardenne Prairie, MO. 1994) p. 18.

70   Meyer, Linda. Wentzville Journal. *The Civil War Revisited*. Vol. 40-Num. 44-June 2, 2002. (The Suburban Journals Publications, St. Louis, MO. 2002) p. Front page.

71   Couch, Ernie. (compilation) *Missouri Trivia*. (Rutledge Hall Press, Nashville, TN, 1992) p. 91.

However, because of strong local sympathy for the Confederate cause, the Missouri River valley heartland became known as "Little Dixie."[72] Before the war ended, 27,000 Missourians, both military and civilian would die.[73]

Ironically, it was during the Civil War, that the phrase, "In God We Trust" began to appear on United States coins.[74]

Flames of hatred

The diverse opinions on slavery couldn't have been more apparent than on the first Sunday of April 1862 when a small group of Union soldiers, possibly from nearby Cottleville, and Judge Krekel's Home Guard, approached Dardenne Church, just before worship services began and asked if they could worship with the congregation. Reverend Watson allowed that if they were willing to leave their weapons outside the church they were welcome to join with the congregation in worshipping God. With Southern sympathizers, and one of St. Charles County's largest slaveholding families among the church members, the incident was surprising—although nothing was said at the time. Despite the circumstances, members of the congregation were equally divided on the issue. Some had family members who had come from Kentucky and Virginia; others supported the Union cause. It wasn't until the following Tuesday evening, April 8th, that the true feelings about the incident became apparent. Some time in the night, the church was set ablaze. The following morning, both the Brick Church and the fence surrounding it were destroyed.[75]

Arson was suspected. Some thought the Union soldiers who had visited; others suspected southern sympathizers. Since there was a large contingent of Southern sympathizers in the Bonhomme area, the Bonhomme Presbyterian Church was immediately padlocked by the authorities for some time. Those guilty of starting the fire were never identified.

Undaunted, the pioneering spirit of Dardenne Presbyterian continued as the congregation worshipped outdoors by substituting their burned church with an "arbor," a primitive shelter to protect worshippers from the elements. Long poles were driven into the ground then boughs of green leaves were placed to form a roof to keep out the sun and light rain. Large enough to house the members during a

72 Ibid., p. 80.
73 Ibid., p. 88.
74 Grun, Bernard. *The Timetables of History.* (Simon and Schuster, New York, NY, 1991) p. 427.
75 Dardenne Presbyterian Archives. *175th Anniversary Celebration-Civil War.* (Dardenne Presbyterian Church, Dardenne Prairie, MO. 1994.) p. 19

service, this arrangement worked well during the late spring, summer and early autumn. During the winter months, if weather permitted travel, members met in each other's homes. According to Elizabeth A. Watson's account in *Heritage and Promise*, the arbor was only used for two summers. Yet generations later the perseverance of the Dardenne family remains. Today, the Dardenne congregation gathers outdoors for services once a year, usually the Sunday closest to the church's anniversary. In doing so, we honor our Dardenne ancestors for their determination to continue in the face of adversity and their dedication to God.

The nation had just begun to heal from the ravages of Civil War, in April of 1865, when stunning news of President Lincoln's death spread throughout the country. We can only imagine how the Dardenne members felt when they learned of his death. They probably knew that the loss of their president would make the task of healing the nation just that much harder. However, the late president's efforts did help ease some of the lingering pain and suffering of the war. Lincoln's legacy to his country lived on in the Thirteenth Amendment to the U.S. Constitution. As a result of his efforts, the reluctant politician from Illinois had abolished slavery in the United States.

Once again, the nation began to focus on the healing process. It also signaled changes within the Dardenne community and a change within Dardenne Presbyterian. After two summers in the brush arbor and several years of meeting in members' homes, the Dardenne members were offered an opportunity to rebuild. In 1868, a new rock church was begun on land located directly across from Rev. Watson's home on the Boones Lick Trail. In 1870, Judge and Mrs. Barton Bates, who owned the land, deeded five acres to Dardenne. Due to the split and subsequent realignment in the Presbyterian church, it was with wisdom and foresight, that Bates stated in the deed "…The Trustees of said property shall in no way or manner be subject to the control, interference, or meddling of any Presbytery, Synod, General Assembly, or other ecclesiastical body." Simply stated, the church owned the land.[76] Bates' reasoning for this particular passage was insightful.

By the end of the Civil War, some of the Presbyterian churches began to realign with others in an effort to heal old wounds. Beginning in 1868, the Presbyterian Church (U.S.A.) Old and New School North united. A substantial number of congregations in the border states of Maryland, Kentucky and Missouri realigned themselves with the Presbyterian Church in the United States (Southern), a successor of the Presbyterian Church of the Confederate States of America, mostly an Old School church. As legal protection, Bates added the clause in case of realignment of the churches. Although the division had occurred thirty years before, Bates would take no chances on the churches reuniting and the land ultimately

---

76 Ibid., p. 21.

being owned by former "New School" advocates.[77] Additionally, Bates was well aware of the law. He was a judge, his father Edward was President Lincoln's Attorney General, and his brother Frederick was Governor of Missouri.

An interesting side note to this deed is that, just like the log cabin church and the Zumwalt deed, the new Rock Church was already built on the land before the Barton deed was written. And just like the Zumwalt deed, it would be several years before it was actually filed at the St. Charles County Courthouse. Although the deed was signed by a judge, it was eight years after the church was built, and six years after the deed was written that in August of 1876, that the deed was finally filed in St. Charles County.

The members built their new church by using the materials at hand. Tradition holds that the rock was quarried from the old site at Dardenne Creek and hauled to the new church site by wagon, and the timber was cut from the surrounding woods. Total cost for erecting the building was $3,835.[78] To this day, the members' craftsmanship speaks for itself. The structure known as the Rock Church still stands and is used on a weekly basis throughout the year. Only a minimum of updating in the 1960's was required to assure continued use. The structure was so well built that it was almost 130 years, in 1996, before the wooden floor had to be replaced.

A gentleman of Scotland arrives

During the church building period of 1868, Rev. Watson realized, with ten children of his own and others in the area, that a school was needed. He built a one-room stone schoolhouse, (with rock from Dardenne creek,) just west of the Watson home at Peach Patch which was across the road from the new church. The teacher, Mr. Adam Lamb, was hired for a stipend of $150 per year. On September 7, 1868, the sixty-four year old Lamb arrived to instruct the Watson children. As time allowed from chores, other children from the neighborhood soon joined classes in the one-room rock schoolhouse across from the new church. Mr. Lamb, originally from Scotland, had taught in Ellisville, High Hill, Fenton and Potosi, before coming to the Watson home.[79]

Well-versed in Greek and Latin, Mr. Lamb subscribed to several daily newspapers from St. Louis. While he kept precise records he had a tendency to be absent minded, but maintained a good humor. During the ten years he was with the

---

77 Ibid., p. 21.
78 Watson, Sally. *Rock Church Presentation*. Carved In Stone Tour-May 13, 2003.
79 Dardenne Presbyterian Church Archives. *175th Anniversary Celebration* (Dardenne Presbyterian Church, Dardenne Prairie, MO. 1994) p. 21.

Watson family, he and Rev. Watson became good friends. It was while young Sam Watson was away at college that a correspondence was begun with Mr. Lamb. One that proved to be insightful into the personalities of both men who would play such an important role in Dardenne's history.[80]

Mr. Lamb was admired and respected by those who knew him, and loved by the Watson children, but sadly, his time with the Watson family and the Dardenne church was brief. When he passed away in 1878 he was buried in the Rock Church Cemetery.

While there is little mention of the women's role within the church during this time, there is one unique reference in Elizabeth A. Watson's *Heritage and Promise*. A receipt was found in Mrs. Thomas (Nannie) Watson's cookbook that showed the women in the church could be very resourceful. They developed a group known as The Mite Society of Dardenne. Their primary function within the church was to clean and prepare for special occasions, but they were not mentioned in positions of authority until 1890. However, in 1870 the Society took on a special role within the church. They saved their money for a year and bought an organ. In July of 1870, they had scraped together the grand total of $26.83 to purchase the instrument.[81]

It was in the 1870's that a friendship developed between Dardenne and our neighbor, Immaculate Conception Church. Originally, Immaculate Conception was a frame building located near the present Feise and Bryan Roads, close to what was the original location of the Boone's Lick Trail. In 1877, six acres was purchased from Judge Barton Bates, for a new Catholic church. Rock was quarried on the Dickherber farm, about 200 yards north of the Orf farm, then hauled across the Orf farm to the new sight on Highway N. The new church was eventually completed and dedicated on June 1, 1897. The friendship and mutual respect between Immaculate Conception and Dardenne has, through the years, continued to grow and strengthen.

In spite of the Civil War, the loss of the church and disruption of regular worship services, the church still claimed eighty-two members and four Elders by 1870.[82] With the completion of the South Dardenne church, Rev. Watson ministered both congregations until 1884, when his son, Rev. Samuel Watson became the installed pastor for the South Dardenne congregation. By the time the church's interior was completed with sparkling kerosene chandeliers and walnut pulpit furniture, with red velvet cushions, it was considered quite elegant

80   Watson, Elizabeth A. *Heritage and Promise: The Story of Dardenne Presbyterian Church.* (Adams Press, Chicago, IL. 1977) p. 236.
81   Ibid., p. 106
82   Ibid., p. 347

for its time. Most of the furnishings were purchased in St. Louis with generous donations from the new members. While the original building plans called for a bell tower, it was many years before the congregation would have a bell and only then because O'Fallon Presbyterian closed its doors.

In April of 1888, Rev. Thomas Watson, the first installed minister regretfully retired due to poor health. He passed away less than two months later. At his funeral on June 3, 1888, T.C. Smith, Robert Branch, and R.P. Farris conducted the service. All three had been close friends of Rev. Watson. Two of the men, Rev. T.C. Smith and Rev. Robert G. Barrett, continued on at Dardenne as Stated Supply ministers through December of that year.[83] Having been the installed pastor of South Dardenne since 1884, Rev. Samuel M. Watson became the Stated Supply pastor for "Old Dardenne" in January of 1889, the year following his father's death. The Dardenne Session invited Rev. Watson to fill the vacant slot and he was installed in 1892. It was a wise move on the part of the Session. For over the next thirty-seven years, the son would prove to be just as dedicated as the father.

83 Dardenne Presbyterian Church *175th Anniversary Celebration* (Dardenne Presbyterian Church, Dardenne Prairie, MO. 1994) p. 22.

Chapter 5

A Journey of Faith: The Third Miracle

For the next four years, Rev. Samuel M. Watson ministered to both South Dardenne and Old Dardenne. In May of 1892, the Session voted to invite him to minister as installed Pastor to Old Dardenne. The Session Book noted that all present voted in favor of the call. The following November, forty-eight years to the month that his father had been installed as pastor at Dardenne, Rev. Samuel Watson became the second installed pastor. He would go on to faithfully serve both congregations until his passing on April 9,1925.[84]

Other than the addition of a wooden narthex on the rock church at "Old Dardenne" in 1890, there was little evidence of church growth during that period of time. This may have been due to a population shift in St. Charles County at the turn of the century. As Protestant families began to move out of the area, Catholic families moved in.

---

84   Dardenne Presbyterian Church. *Session Records, 1892*. (Dardenne Presbyterian Church, Dardenne Prairie, MO. 1892.)

Yet, during the time that Rev. Watson served the churches a number of historic events took place. During his years of service, church members would see the Nobel Prize established, and learn of the Curie's discovery of radium. Technology made giant strides at the turn of the century with the first radio broadcast in 1906. Shortly thereafter telephone service became available in major cities across the country. It's really no wonder few paid attention to a lecture by a little-known Professor A. O. Rankine. The lecture, entitled "Hearing with Light", predicted that in the near future people would be watching and hearing moving pictures. It would be several years before Rankine's prediction would come true and when it did, "talkies" became the rage.[85]

Rev. Samuel McCluer Watson
The Second Installed Pastor of Dardenne
Presbyterian Church—1892–1925

Meet Me In St. Louis

Turn of the century St. Louisans, and those in the surrounding area, found themselves preparing for the Louisiana Exposition, known generally as the St. Louis World's Fair. As work began, famous St. Louisans made their opinions known on areas that needed improvement. Until March 23, 1904, St. Louis' murky tap water was a civic shame. Mark Twain wrote of it: "Every tumbler holds an acre in solution. If you will let your glass stand half an hour you can separate land from water as easy as Genesis…" The city needed clean water for the upcoming fair. By the fair opening in May, Mr. John P. Wixford, a St. Louis chemical engineer had solved the problem.[86]

---

85 Grun, Bernard. *The Timetables of History* (Simon and Schuster, New York, NY. 1991) p. 488

86 Stadler, Frances Hurd. *St. Louis Day by Day.* (Simon and Schuster, New York, NY. 1991) p 55.

On April 30, 1904, amid a spectacular opening ceremony which included William Howard Taft, the long-awaited Louisiana Exposition—The St. Louis World's Fair was officially opened.[87]

One of the many highlights of the fair came on August 12th of that year when a cavalcade of 70 automobiles, driven 1,477 miles from Boston, arrived so fairgoers could see "the automobiles of the future." The fourteen-day trip included driving over rutted roads and cornfields. The parade of motorcars drove through the fairgrounds and extra excitement was provided with a "salute from the 'tooter' of every automobile." The mayor of Poughkeepsie, New York sent this greeting to the mayor of St. Louis: "In this age of progress, I cannot find a more fitting method of conveying this city's respects for the Exposition City than by means of these most modern couriers."[88]

Sadly, the thirty-seven year time period when Rev. Watson ministered to both churches was also a time of loss and tragedy for the country. America went to war with Spain, the Titanic sank, and everybody was singing "Over There" as young soldiers left for Europe to fight in the war that was supposed to end all wars, World War I.

Lost amid the events of the time was one story about the Bible that the newspapers didn't even mention. Few knew that in the Fourteenth century a bible had cost the equivalent of $2,000. Thanks to Johannes Guttenberg the price dropped sharply to $500 in the 1450's. By the seventeenth century a bible could be purchased for $100. However, by 1925, just about everybody could afford one when the price reached $3.00.[89]

---

87 Ibid., p. 79.
88 Ibid., p. 153.
89 Grun, Bernard. The Timetables of History. (Simon and Schuster, New York, NY. 1991) p. 459

Dardenne Presbyterian Rock Church in Dardenne Prairie Showing Original Wooden Narthex
Photo courtesy of Sally Watson

The Quiet Time

When Rev. Watson passed away in April of 1925, Dardenne members had no way of knowing it would be forty-five years before their church would see another installed pastor. During this time, regular weekly Sunday services would cease and the membership would drop to two members, Mr. Hunter Hutchings and Miss Emily Watson. Not until the South Dardenne Church in the 1940's was sold to the United States government and the remaining members joined Hutchings and Watson would Old Dardenne begin to grow again. The ebb and flow of the population shift in St. Charles County, such as had occurred at the turn of the century, had begun again, and had a notable impact on the church as well as the community. St. Charles County was not alone in this phenomenon. A general population shift from the country to the city was proving to be a difficult time in rural areas across America. During the interim from Watson's death to the installation of another pastor, stated supply pastors and lay leaders provided for the spiritual needs of the dwindling congregation. Worship services were held once a month during the year, except during the winter months. Although the few members did their best to keep the church and grounds maintained, it was becoming a more difficult job as the years passed.

Several stated supply ministers shared the duties and filled the pulpit during this time: Usually, Dr. Calvin Colby, pastor of the First Presbyterian Church of St. Charles, the Rev. Fred Reeves and Rev. Glen Williams, both of the South Dardenne Church at Howell, Missouri would be available. Occasionally, other pastors would fill the Dardenne pulpit as a guest pastor.

Yet, as the little church struggled, the world around it continued to evolve. Where the automobile had been the machine of wonder at the World's Fair, now Americans were in awe of the airplane and with it came a new type of hero: the pilot. On May 20, 1927, Charles Augustus Lindbergh left New York for a non-stop flight to Paris. At stake was a $25,000 reward from Raymond Orteig.

Backed by nine St. Louis businessmen, Lindbergh, in his Spirit of St. Louis, was spotted off the Irish coast, then over England and finally, crossing the English channel. He landed in LeBourget Field in Paris the next day. America had a new hero.[90]

When the economic depression swept the nation in the 1930's, most families were doing well to keep food on the table, let alone find money to make improvements to their churches. However, a blessing was about to be bestowed from a most unusual source. On April 6, 1931, about 1,000 gathered at the Odeon Theater in St. Louis to hear city leaders discuss ways to ease unemployment in St. Louis. Eventually, a fund of $300,000 was collected from local religious leaders to supplement city aid to the unemployed, then estimated to be between 75,000 and 100,000.[91]

Additionally, the 1940 Act of Congress known as, "Expediting Production" didn't resemble a blessing for our church at the time, but it did bring notable changes to St. Charles County. The Act meant, among other things, land could be taken for the manufacturing of munitions. The Weldon Spring Ordinance Works, established in St. Charles County, meant buying a large tract of land and evacuating, then leveling, everything within its perimeter. This project began to provide some employment and needed cash for families in the area. Although the Army Corps of Engineers supervised the job, local labor was assigned to complete the project. Soon, local merchants began to see a profit and local churches saw more money in the collection plates on Sunday. Perhaps the most important change to the area, as far as the Old Dardenne Church was concerned, was the sale of our sister church, known as South Dardenne

Part of the area included in the evacuation was the town of Howell (formerly known as Mechanicsville), Hamburg and the South Dardenne Church. This

90   Stadler, Frances Hurd. St. Louis Day by Day. (The Patrice Press, St. Louis, MO. 1991) p. 94.
91   Ibid., p. 64.

property also included the original Dardenne Creek church site and the cemetery where most of the founding members rested. By November 1940, the South Dardenne Church authorized the sale of its church property to the Government for $7,305.42. The elegant walnut furnishings, kerosene chandeliers, an old upright piano of undetermined date, and $600 cash were given to Old Dardenne.

In the process of closing, eleven members strengthened the congregation by transferring to the Old Dardenne Rock Church, which helped keep Old Dardenne alive. According to Jane Elzea's history of the church there were only two members at Old Dardenne at that time, Mr. Hunter Hutchings and Miss Emily Watson.[92]

The additional funds transferred to Old Dardenne and an improving economy in the county, assisted in much needed repairs that had been delayed due to lack of funding. Members realized that additional money and a few more members could help the church continue.[93]

Despite economic downturns, the closing of South Dardenne and the rationing of products during World War II, more than one hundred people met to celebrate the 125th anniversary of Dardenne Presbyterian church on September 24, 1944. The congregation produced a memorable celebration. A special commemorative booklet was published with a history written by Mrs. William C. Wilson. The booklet also contained a Roster of Attendance and a copy of the sermon given that day by the guest speaker, Dr. Walter M. Langtry.[94]

At the 130th anniversary celebration, in July 1949, Dardenne held a reunion. Of the seventy-seven attending, many were descendants of families who made up both the Old Dardenne and South Dardenne congregations. Immaculate Conception, the Catholic church located about one mile west of Dardenne, opened its doors and provided space for a celebratory dinner. Additionally, their kindness was extended by not only providing the kitchen and dining space, but preparing the meal and serving it as well.

Despite these celebrations, church membership at Dardenne, continued to decline due to the changing economic conditions within the community. If not for a few steadfast members, Dardenne probably would not have survived. Fewer family farms were to be found as many people moved closer to the St. Louis area seeking more reliable methods, other than farming, to support their families.

The Dardenne Prairie community was still a small country area even as late as the 1950's. Boone's Lick Road, also known as Missouri Highway N or The Old

92 Elzea, Jane. The History of Dardenne Presbyterian Church. (Dardenne Prairie, MO. 1962)
93 Dardenne Presbyterian Church, 175th Anniversary Celebration. (Dardenne Presbyterian Church, Dardenne Prairie, MO. 1994.) p. 23.
94 Ibid., p. 23.

Trail, was still a gravel road until the early 1960's. Church services were usually held once a month in good weather. In rainy weather, automobiles had difficulty turning into the driveway from Highway N. Often a Stated Supply pastor was available but, at times, a lay person was called upon to lead the service. Still, love and hope among the few remaining members strengthened the bond of fellowship.

By April of 1953 only fourteen members remained. On April 3rd they submitted a letter to the stated Clerk of the Presbytery requesting that Elder Charles R. Watson be appointed Lay Leader for the church. Three weeks later, a letter from the Presbytery arrived stating that Elder Watson was now Lay Leader Watson. While he could conduct services and lead Session, only an ordained minister could perform the sacraments. Mr. Watson, son of Rev. Samuel Watson and grandson of Rev. Thomas Watson, worked diligently to restore Old Dardenne. Although allied with the sister church for most of his life, he and his wife, Allene, transferred to Old Dardenne when South Dardenne had closed. He served Dardenne until 1956.

Other than the contribution of furniture and chandeliers from South Dardenne, the Rock Church had changed little since the 1890's when the wooden narthex was added to the front of the building. But that didn't mean the church was dormant. There were still a few faithful who were determined to keep the doors open. At this point, the church struggled to hold four services a year. Usually this happened only in good weather when a guest minister or lay person was available. Yet, despite their dedication, the church continued to falter. According to the Elzea history, the church was closed for several years. It reopened on April 29, 1962.

The 1960's presented new challenges the members had never faced before. Instigated by outside sources, the dilemmas would test their mettle, and through the course, strengthen the congregation's resolve to carry on the mission work of Dardenne Presbyterian Church. At one point, the church membership was so low that Mr. Mayburn Snyder and Mr. Hutchings held the positions of both Elder and Deacon.

The wake-up call

The nine remaining members were still committed to spreading the Gospel and continued in their steadfast loyalty to the church. Indeed, for several years, the small membership had encouraged a close fellowship. While the members remained constant and dedicated, a small drama began to unfold which would continue for several years and, in the end, would prove to be a turning point for the declining church. On June 5, 1961, a member of Dardenne, Earle Tyler Castlio, passed away

While Ms. Castlio had bequeathed, $30,000, mostly in land, to be divided equally among three entities, there was a stipulation for Dardenne members that was difficult to meet. The bequest, which consisted mainly of real estate, was equally divided between Dardenne Presbyterian Church, The Child Evangelism Fellowship and Billy Graham Evangelistic Association. While there were no conditions or limitations required of the latter two, there was one prerequisite required of Ms. Castlio's church. The Will stated that Dardenne, "…shall share in such residue only if within nine months after my death it shall have a full-time pastor and be holding church services regularly, and if not, all of the residue shall go to the said Billy Graham Evangelistic Association and Child Evangelism Fellowship in equal shares."[95]

For many years, the practical solution for worship services at Dardenne had been to hold monthly service during good weather when a stated supply pastor was available. It was not until the last day of the nine-month deadline that arrangements were made to hold services more often. During that time the pastor, Dr. Stuart Salmon, served full-time to the Overland congregation and had held only four services at Dardenne during the nine-month period. Two services had been presided over by laymen. Dr. Salmon and one other pastor had led the other two. Dardenne records indicated that the governing body of three members had met only three times during 1961. The nine-month deadline for qualification, according to the Will, was March 5, 1962. At the March 4, 1962 meeting the governing body set up a plan for regular services, which were to be held once a month beginning in April of that year.

A St. Louis Post Dispatch article from that time noted that regularly scheduled worship services didn't start again until the end of June 1962. The July 9th article, noted that the worship service the writer had attended was the first in almost a year. It went on to note that regular weekly services had stopped in 1952. A flattering article by an unnamed staff writer, it emphasized the unique history and provided colorful anecdotes. Although the article didn't mention the lawsuit, it seemed as though the writer sought to assist Dardenne in its cause. Whatever the purpose, the final decision rested with the higher court.[96]

Eventually, the local court ruled against Dardenne and the matter was appealed to the Missouri Supreme Court. The Supreme Court stayed the decision and again the church lost. What both courts failed to consider was the phrasing in the Castlio will and the circumstances. First, regular weekly services had ended ten years earlier. Until 1961, with Castlio's passing, services were held on the last Sunday of each month in good weather. Another problem was the driveway to

---

95 South Western Reporter, 2d Series. Smith v. Dardenne Presbyterian Church. (Cite as 378 S.W. 2d) p. 466.
96 St. Louis Post Dispatch-July 9, 1962-Special Correspondent. *92-Year-Old Dardenne Church Is Scene of Services Again.*

the church. Although the church was only about 75 feet from a state-improved road, it was difficult for cars to leave the road and drive up the steep incline to the church. The church did not have a paved parking lot or driveway at that time.

Dardenne's position maintained that Rev. Salmon was a full-time pastor supplied by the Presbytery to serve the congregation once a month and monthly services were considered the norm at Dardenne. Additionally, they argued, Ms. Castlio's intention for "holding regular services" was based on that practice of monthly services, not weekly services. Ultimately, the decision of both courts seemed to be a matter of interpretation and Dardenne did not receive the money.

A Call To Action

In a touching letter to Rev. Billy Graham in December 1962, just before they were to appear in court in St. Charles, Rev. Salmon wrote explaining Dardenne's position. His closing remarks to Dr. Graham revealed his hope for Dardenne's future. "Another Ruling Elder is to be elected in a Congregational meeting following the service on December 30. Four new members were received at our service on November 25. The future is bright with promise, since several very large housing developments are in various stages of planning, development, and even sales already, in the close vicinity, and this church has Comity rights in this area."[97] (See Chapter 9, page 65.)

Rev. Salmon and the Dardenne family understood what the Courts had failed to see—the church's future was bright because their faith in God gave them hope that better times were ahead. Yet, the loss of the money from the Castlio bequest proved a hidden blessing. The members were determined to keep the doors open and willing to look at any possibility to do so. The loss seemed to be a clarion call to be about God's work. At one point, Rev. Salmon contacted developer Ira L. Nathan who was developing a new project in the St. Charles County area to be known as Lake St. Louis. Mr. Nathan's letter located in the Dardenne archives indicated that Rev. Salmon was interested in developing a new site for the church.[98] There is no follow-up paperwork, save a newspaper map of the "new development" and the one letter from Mr. Nathan seems to be a reply to Rev. Salmon's inquiry. Nathan's letter offers a piece of land in Lake St. Louis at a reduced rate until January 1, 1964.

Meanwhile, Rev. Salmon was instrumental in generating interest in Dardenne among other, more affluent churches, during a crucial time. His efforts were reinforced by the generous moral support and financial contribution from the

---

97 Salmon, Rev. Stuart H. Correspondence to Rev. Dr. Billy Graham-December 20, 1965.
98 Nathan. Ira L. to Rev. Stuart H. Salmon—October 15, 1963.

congregation of Central Presbyterian Church in Clayton, Missouri. The additional funds provided the church with a well, plumbing, electric lamps and a gas furnace to replace the wood burning stoves. The wooden narthex was replaced with a new brick entrance and porch. A side door was installed in the west wall. Dr. Salmon contributed the carved walnut Celtic cross behind the pulpit as well as the cross above the porch entrance. Those involved in the remodeling were careful to retain as much of the historical character of the building as possible.[99]

By 1965, Dardenne's future did indeed look brighter for the church. In that year, Sally Watson and Allene Watson became the first women Elders in the church. That summer, Mr. Charles Bunce, his wife June and their children moved into the area. By December, Mr. Bunce was ordained an Elder and the membership had increased to seventeen.

The Sunday School classes were reorganized and meeting weekly by June. Weekly church services were held every Sunday for the first time since 1952. Within a few years, membership had steadily increased and those who came and stayed were eager to help.

---

99   Pritchard, Claude H. Correspondence to Rev. Staurt H. Salmon-February 18,1965.

Chapter 6

The New Mission Field

During the mid-60's, a survey was conducted in the Dardenne Prairie-O'Fallon area which determined that Dardenne Presbyterian had "no future" in the community. This, the survey concluded, was due to the large Catholic population in the area. This information coupled with the loss of the Castlio bequest might have caused most churches to consider closing the doors. Yet, prayerful consideration of the facts by the congregation had the opposite effect.

Dardenne had one thing in its favor that other Protestant churches could not claim. It was centrally located in St. Charles County and suddenly found itself surrounded by a building boom. Located halfway between Interstate highways 40 and 70, the central location in St. Charles County offered easy access for a growing community of newly built businesses, subdivisions and schools.

This building trend continued into the late 1990's as witnessed with the WingHaven development. Additionally, the Page Avenue Extension is to pass near the church when completed. While it might have been true that Dardenne had no future as a neighborhood church the basic strategy as a regional church began to form. With an attitude that "St. Charles County is our mission field" Dardenne members, persistent as ever, went to work.

Perhaps it was because of Dardenne's determination to remain open, that in 1966 the Presbytery sent a full-time Stated Supply pastor. Dr. Herbert Watson was retired from regular pastoral ministry when he was appointed by the Presbytery to be Supply for Dardenne. A descendant of both Rev. Thomas Watson, the first installed pastor at Dardenne and Rev. Samuel M. Watson, the second installed pastor, Dr. Watson returned the church to regular weekly services, and organized church boards. Since the survey of 1965 suggested a regional church strategy would work best, Dr. Watson set about making the name of Dardenne Presbyterian known throughout the area as church members began visiting the distant subdivisions. Dardenne had been Rev. Watson's boyhood home and he had spent much of his ministry involved in church development. Working the subdivisions brought about another community outreach program-one designed to visit prospective new members. At one point, the Elders and Deacons and their spouses would divide into teams and visit the area. Today, Dardenne members know a similar program as "The Minutemen."

"The Minutemen" are the Dardenne welcoming committee. When visitors arrive at Dardenne for worship, they are encouraged to sign the notebook located in each pew. After the service, The Minutemen visit the homes of first-time attendees, tell them about the church, answer any questions they may have, but most importantly, let them know that they are welcome. It is an opportunity to let visitors to the church know they have a place at Dardenne if they choose. Over the years, untold numbers of visitors have gone on to become members of Dardenne as a result of a Minuteman visit. In 1998, a new tradition began with the Minutemen. Each home visited is gifted with a small loaf of home-baked bread as a welcome gift.

However, in 1967 new leadership was required to continue this evangelizing mission and new growth within the church. After serving only eight months, Dr. Watson retired and moved to Auxvasse, Missouri. Although he had served only a short while, his efforts strengthened the church by establishing an ongoing outreach program. In that same year, Dr. Stuart Salmon retired from the ministry as well. His legacy to Dardenne, among other things, includes the Celtic crosses he carved which are seen above the porch and in the nave of the Rock Church. Together, Revs. Watson and Salmon will be remembered for their leadership and organized effort to launch the "regional concept" for Dardenne. Thanks to their efforts, church membership grew rapidly in the time they were associated with the church.

With Dr. Salmon and Dr. Watson's retirements, Dardenne received guidance from Lay Leader, Mr. Charles M. Bunce. Elected to the Session, he was ordained an

Rev. Charles Bunce
Pastor of Dardenne Presbyterian 1970–1973

Elder on Dec.11, 1965. Mr. Bunce was formerly a pastor for churches in Kentucky and Maryland. In May of 1967, when Rev. Watson retired, Mr. Bunce assumed the pastoral work. By October 10, 1970, he became Rev. Charles Bunce when he was ordained and installed as pastor of Dardenne. By January 10th of the following year, he had resigned his position with the St. Louis Post-Dispatch as Religion Editor and began full-time duties as Dardenne pastor. Rev. Bunce was only the third installed pastor in the 150-year history of the church. Much loved by a congregation who called him, "Charles," Rev. Bunce would lead the church during a time that would see the completion of one building, the start of another and the renovation of a third all within a few years.[100]

Rev. Bunce launched a number of activities within the church that appealed to just about every age group. Among them were Vacation Bible School for the youngsters and The Presbyteens for the young adults. Three Presbyterian Women's groups, or Circles, were begun. Today, that number has grown to six Circles. Their dedication and service to the church has continued to provide valuable services to the church and community for several decades. Additional activities were added to meet the demands of a growing congregation. A children's choir, and more youth group activities provided for the younger members.

The Dardennaire

For a true picture of church growth and the enthusiasm of church members to serve, The Dardennaire, the church newsletter, provides insight to a growing church. In an early one-page edition, members made a statement about missions that read, "We look forward to the day that Dardenne can provide for missions

---

100 The Dardennaire Collection. January 1971-1973. Dardenne Presbyterian Church Archives, Dardenne Prairie, MO.

and other benevolence causes." While the Dardennaire most assuredly had foreign missions in mind with that statement, it was evident that the church was meeting the needs of missions closer to home. The day arrived shortly thereafter when the women of the church set about to raise money for a special project. Within a few months, they made a contribution to St. Peters Elementary School. Word had reached church members that two students were in need of kidney dialysis and the women of Dardenne had lent a helping hand. Such was the way then without forming a committee; church members would quietly set about to help somebody in need. There were several instances of the church donating food, clothing, or money to people in the community. More often than not, the recipients of this Christian kindness weren't even members of the church.

The Dardennaire began as a one-page newsletter to the forty-seven members of Dardenne in 1967. This was an increase of thirty members in six months time. It was a good start for a country church of nine members just five years earlier and an incredible feat for a church struggling to stay afloat yet invest its time and energy in establishing a regional church image and forming various groups and ministries for its congregation. The first Dardennaire issue appeared in February of that year but it was several months before the next issue was published. As church membership grew, so did the news.

Announcements for volunteers to help with various chores around the church, the subject of the next sermon or which members were traveling was all included. In September 1967 the Dardennaire proudly announced that the Building Fund started at Homecoming Sunday that month had yielded a total of $88.50. Eventually additional contributions added new pews in the Rock Church, and robes for a growing choir.

The Building Fund to construct Watson Hall, begun in September of 1967, was growing slowly when in November of 1968, at the same time of the church anniversary celebration, a new source of help arrived. The Central Presbyterian Church offered Dardenne a 2-for-1 challenge in a three-year campaign. Dardenne had determined that an adequate building would cost about $100,000 dollars. Central would provide $50,000 dollars if Dardenne could raise $25,000. The balance of $25,000 would be acquired with long term financing. Several months later, when Dardenne reached the $5,000 mark, Central presented a check for $10,000.[101]

Every possible method was employed to gain the needed $25,000. That year at Christmas, members even sent one greeting card to the church and sent the money they would have spent on cards to the church Building Fund. The following year, in 1968, the Bonhomme Presbyterian congregation contributed $500 to the building fund. With a second lease on life, Dardenne moved into a growth

---

101 Dardennaire Collection January 1971-January 1973. (Dardenne Presbyterian Church, Dardenne Prairie, MO. 1973.) pp. 1-25.

phase and the Dardenne family was willing to utilize whatever talents were needed to make continued growth a success.

Watson Hall Under Construction on West Side of the Rock Church.
Note the two trailers donated by Synod on the east side of the Rock Church.
The new building was dedicated on December 13, 1970

A flurry of activity ushered in 1968. In the spring, the sign in front of the church was installed and dedicated to Earl Sutton, a faithful officer of the church for many years. A second trailer arrived to provide additional space as the church had rapidly outgrown the first trailer from the Synod and was immediately put to good use. That summer, the church purchased five acres of land west of the church. All signs indicated that Dardenne was once again moving forward.

The Planning committee began to make arrangements for the 150th anniversary of the church and the 100th anniversary of the Rock Church. Although members had hoped to have 150 members by its 150th birthday, they did reach 106 members. Dardenne was rapidly leaving behind the "little country church" image. The church had good reason to celebrate its 150th Anniversary and the 100th anniversary of the Rock Church with a 2-year long celebration. Both the Post Dispatch and the Wentzville Union presented articles about the celebration and the year-long events that were to begin November 22nd and extended through September 1969. "Old Dardenne in A New Day" was the theme. The speaker at the opening event, a dinner at Immaculate Conception, was Rev. Frank Caldwell—the Director of the Presbyterian Foundation in Charlotte, NC. According to a Post-Dispatch article, Rev. Caldwell was considered one of the finest preachers in the Presbyterian Church.[102]

The growth continues

As Thanksgiving approached that year, plans were made to return one of the trailers to the Synod and to sell the other one. With the new building nearing completion, they were no longer needed. The dedication of the new building was delayed for a few weeks due to an electrical problem.

On December 13, 1970, over 160 church members and friends of the church gathered for the dedication of Watson Hall. Rev. Lindy M. Cannon, Moderator of the Presbytery, dedicated the new building to Rev. Thomas Watson, Rev. Sam Watson, Ruling Elder Charles Ruffner Watson, and in honor of the Rev. Dr. Herbert H. Watson. Those participating in the dedication service, according to the program, are names that are still well known in the church. The recently ordained, Rev. Charles Bunce, Mr. Clyde Mouser and Ms. Sally A. Watson.

Although Watson Hall was evidence that Dardenne was growing, one could also look at the activity within the congregation. Although Dardenne had only nine members in 1965, by 1971, more than a dozen committees were needed to oversee the operations of the church.

In the spring of 1971, the church purchased the Manse at 18 Knollwood Circle near Highways N and 94 close to St. Charles in the Greenwood Subdivision. The price was $25,000. In March of 1973, the house would be sold for $30,000 because of the constant repairs.

By May of 1972, a second building campaign was underway. Initially known as the Education Building it would eventually house the Sunday School classes and what is known as the kitchen. The women of the church found a unique way to furnish the kitchen with the needed equipment. A list of needed items was posted and everybody was invited to a "Kitchen Shower." Similar to a Bridal Shower or a Baby Shower, invited guests brought items from the list. This plan proved so successful that the following year, the church library would offer a variation of it with a Book Shower.

The church library service began with Sue Spellman as librarian. Two years later, Madelyn Hopper filled the position. Housed in one of the donated trailers, the library consisted of just a few books and the Vacation Bible School Curriculum, which was kept each year for reference. In order to expand the library collection,

102 St. Louis Post Dispatch (Edition, page and date unknown—Dardenne archives)

the Presbyterian Women held a "Book Shower" in October of 1973, as donated books began to arrive, boxes and paper bags full of books were stacked in the corner of one of the trailers until they could be catalogued. During the next two decades, the library seemed to expand with the church and eventually called several locations home: two different locations within Watson Hall, the room next to the Pastors office and finally the conference room next to the church office. During most of this time, the library was open on Sunday mornings and Wednesday evenings to accommodate members who sought additional knowledge on the Christian faith.

During that time, the church continued offering assistance to three area families with car repairs, food, bedding, clothing and financial assistance with utility bills.[105] A variety of projects kept church teens busy. The Presbyteens, as they were known, were offered a variety of missions close to home. The December 1972 copy of the Dardennaire noted they were using their spare time that month to cut firewood for area families who could not otherwise afford fuel to heat their homes.

The first recorded instance of mission trips is in the March, Dardennaire of 1972 when eight young people are listed as preparing for a mission trip to Guatemala. Apparently there was interest in foreign mission work long before the funding became available. An earlier Dardennaire lists a Damian Obika from Biafra speaking to the group on May 3, 1970.[103]

Begun in 1972, renovation of the Rock Church was a thorough job. Included were new pews, chancel rail, lectern, and carpet. Floor repairs, electrical work, and paint were included in the work projects. Upon completion, a rededication of the old Rock Church was celebrated as members and friends of the church gathered to hear Dr. Frank L. "Bullet" McCluer, Retired. President of Lindenwood University, former moderator of the Synod of Missouri and Vice Moderator of the General Assembly deliver the sermon.

As the church continued to grow, so did the responsibilities. Dardenne had grown from a membership of nine members in 1965 to 292 members in 1973.

In April of 1973, Rev. Bunce asked the Session to consider bringing in a "promising young seminary student" as a part-time assistant to lighten his workload. Perhaps one of his last written messages to the congregation best sums up Rev. Bunce's life at Dardenne. In the April 25, 1973 Dardennaire, he noted to church members that Easter was the beginning of preparation for Pentecost. A time, he noted, "when the Holy Spirit came to the Church with power, bringing to the Christians the knowledge of the continual presence of the Risen Christ." Rev. Bunce continued, "With a glorious Easter behind us, we should now reach out

---

103 *The Dardennaire*, March 16, 1972 (p. 1) and May 3, 1970.(p. 1) (Dardenne Presbyterian Church, Dardenne Prairie, MO. 1973)

and expand our program of worship, prayer, Bible study, witness and service as never before. Who knows what God may have in mind for Dardenne Church in the weeks and months ahead?"[104]

By the following month, Rev. Bunce was placed on sick leave. On June 27, 1973, "Charles," as his Dardenne family knew him, had passed away.

In the August Dardennaire that year, probably the first published after his passing, the writer noted that the most lasting monument to his memory would be a growing, living memorial—an active church. "Not just a plaque that gathers cobwebs." The writer went on to offer a suggestion to achieve that goal. "...We fill our pews, we visit our sick, we welcome the new, we keep preaching God's word, we pray together, and we work together to build Dardenne Presbyterian Church."[105] Apparently Dardenne members took these words to heart for forty years later their memorial to Charles Bunce is a thriving, active regional leader in the community.

---

104 Bunce, Rev. Charles M. *The Dardennaire,* April 25, 1973. (Dardenne Presbyterian Church, Dardenne Prairie, MO. 1973.) p. 1.
105 Author unknown. *The Dardennaire*, August 18, 1973. (Dardenne Presbyterian Church, Dardenne Prairie, MO. 1973.) p. 1.

Chapter 7

Transition and Renewal

A New Era Begins

By the following year, it was evident there was a new strength; a renewed vitality that seemed to be moving through the church. Although the church still mourned the loss of Charles Bunce, the late winter and early spring of 1974 brought more changes to Dardenne.

The congregation knew it needed to fill the position left vacant with the passing of Rev. Bunce. This, in itself was not an easy task. With the assistance of Rev. Gary Myers of Bonhomme Presbyterian who served as Moderator for the Session, they set about to find a new pastor for the growing congregation. In April of 1974, the Session called Rev. Thomas L. Sale to minister to the needs of Dardenne. Installed on June 2, 1974, Rev. Sale would lead Dardenne through a new adventure, one of unprecedented growth. Continuing in the footsteps of Charles Bunce, he piloted Dardenne into an even larger development phase. In the 155-year history of the church, Rev. Sale was only the fourth installed pastor called to serve the congregation and he now led a 186-member church.

Under his able leadership, the church would see phenomenal growth with membership in excess of one thousand for the first time in its history. St. Charles

County was growing also as a new population shift found many families leaving North county and the general St. Louis area for the St. Charles/O'Fallon community. Additionally, the St. Charles County area was convenient for the expanding industrial base that was building around the airport and the McDonnell Douglas—now Boeing—complex.

The Annual Ice Cream Social, begun in 1967, was reinstated. It has become a much-anticipated event among the congregation and friends of the church. The first was held on an August Sunday on the church lawn with members encouraged to bring ice-cream freezers for a summer afternoon of music, fun and homemade ice cream. Each

Rev. Thomas L. Sale
Fourth Installed Dardenne Pastor 1973—1997

year something more was added to the event. Now, the Annual Ice Cream Social offers church members and guests far more than ice cream, cookies and socializing. Through the years, entertainment has come to include hilarious old-time melodrama by The Fellowship Players that rivals the best histrionics ever offered by the now defunct Goldenrod Showboat.

In May of 1977, the congregation would see an additional worship service, at 9:45 a.m., added to accommodate the larger congregation. By the summer, a new organ was dedicated. More changes and additions were on the way as an adult choir was reformed and plans were underway for additional children's choirs for each age level.

Dardenne has been blessed with talented choir directors. Following Phil Salvati, Mrs. Karla Leigh became the choir director in the mid-70's. She and her husband Jerry and their children were devoted members of Dardenne for over 20 years. For many years she devotedly oversaw all phases of the music ministry.

Stephanie Liesman, wife of Youth Leader, Steve Liesman, and daughter-in-law to Arnie and Doris Liesman followed Karla Leigh. Mrs. Liesman retired in order to start a family in 2002. Once again, Dardenne was blessed when the Stacey Burchette family arrived. They have also been very active in the Mission program.

Unless you are a choir participant, most members only see the end result of the choir director's efforts on Sunday morning. Both the director and choir members spend long hours each week preparing for the Sunday morning presentation. In addition, they prepare music for additional programs, such as the annual Christmas program, the Mission Conference and this year's 185th Anniversary program. Over the years, each choir director has left his or her imprint on the choir. Additionally, each has left warm memories of their efforts with each member.

By the 1980's yet a third service at 8:00 a.m. was added to the Sunday worship schedule to accommodate the growing congregation. It was during this building phase that another annual practice was re-established.

While an annual outdoor worship service had been held for many years, the custom had been discontinued as membership dwindled. Usually held in September on the Sunday closest to the founding date, at least two of the three services are held outdoors. While in doing so, the congregation is reminded of the beauty of God's world, its primary purpose is to commemorate the perseverance of the earlier church members who continued a church in a brush arbor, when they had no building.

In 1977, Elizabeth A. Watson published her *Heritage and Promise*: A Story of Dardenne Presbyterian Church and Its Community. Although a member of St. Charles Presbyterian, Mrs. Watson was the first to publish an historical account about the Dardenne church. Having grown up in the Dardenne Prairie and Howell area, she was familiar with many of the families and the colorful history of the county. Related to the Watson family through marriage, she understood the interaction of community and country church. Additionally, as a member of the St. Charles and Missouri Historical Societies, she had access to significant information concerning the early days of the church. Related to the Watson family through marriage, she understood the interaction of the church and its community. The Watson family archives produced some never-before-seen photographs of the Watson family and church members from earlier days. Several copies of her work, a labor of love, are kept in the Thomas M. Sale library at Dardenne and are still used for historical reference.

Dardenne's Renaissance

It would seem that by 1962, as the membership dwindled to nine members and the church faced economic hardship, Dardenne was perilously close to closing. However, God in his infinite wisdom had other plans. Within two decades Dardenne members would renovate the Rock Church, build Watson, Salmon and Robinson Halls and erect the new Brick Church. Following in the footsteps of their nineteenth century counterparts. Dardenne volunteers completed the majority of the work.

If the nineteenth century Dardenne church family exemplified the pioneering spirit, then the mark of twentieth century Dardenne members had to be one of "do-it-yourself" volunteers. This became evident when the church entered its unprecedented building phase that began in the 1960's and continued through 2002. With the exception of the Christian Life Center, the majority of work was done by volunteer labor from members in the church.

The first project was a renovation of Watson Hall, then the volunteers' abilities were really tested with the building of the present "Brick Church." After the shell was in place and the wiring was complete, volunteers began to apply the finishing touches. In February 1974, the church started a memorial fund for a bell tower. We already owned a bell which had a history of its own. When O'Fallon Presbyterian closed its doors in 1947, their church bell was gifted to Dardenne. When the bell tower was completed in the new Brick Church, it was decided the tower would be dedicated to the memory of Rev. Charles Bunce. The Charles Bunce Memorial Bell Tower was completed and the building was dedicated on September 15, 1985.

The New Brick Church Nearing Completion

While the per capita income of Missourians was only $13,657 at the time, necessary funding was flowing in to Dardenne.[106] Throughout this expansion effort and unprecedented growth, Rev. Sale continued his efforts to establish a written history of the church and to place the Rock Church on the historic registry with the Presbyterian Church. Several letters over a four-year period, indicate that Rev. Sale continued his search for information on those involved with Dardenne and its inception. In the Dardenne archives, letters from the Presbyterian Historical Society of Philadelphia, Andover-Newton Theological School and The State Historical Society of Missouri, indicate Rev. Sale's continued efforts to locate information. Unfortunately, the Presbyterian Historical Society of Philadelphia declined saying that not enough evidence was available to support naming the Rock Church as an historical site.

---

106 Couch, Ernie. (compilation) *Missouri Trivia*. (Rutledge Hall Pres, Nashville, TN. 1991) p. 79.

Meanwhile, the church found yet another way to provide for the needs of the community. After careful deliberation by Rev. Sale and the Session, a preschool was begun. As a fitting tribute to the much-loved teacher of the Watson children, the Adam Lamb Preschool opened in 1987. With Karen Loechner as Education Director, the current enrollment has grown to over two hundred children. Young minds are engaged daily with Bible lessons, crafts, and circle time where they learn about the calendar, weather, Pledge of Allegiance and other activities to engage active youngsters.

Starship Dardenne

The Lloyd Daugherty Memorial Organ. Led by Jerry Leigh, project chair, the system was completed by Dardenne volunteers.

In November of 1995, ten years after the completion of the Brick Church, the Dardenne family came together to donate their time and abilities for yet another "do-it-yourself" project. In doing so, they implemented what may well be one of the largest volunteer organ construction projects of its kind in the United States. With the assistance of only one consultant, Mr. Marlin Mackley, the members set out to build a 65-rank, 3,500-pipe organ—complete with a computerized console.[107]

In 1981, church member Lloyd Daugherty had donated $35,000 for a pipe organ system. By 1995, the fund had grown to $65,000.00. The new Brick Church and the nave had been built with a pipe organ system in mind. In 1985, Rev. Tom Sale had even included the necessary pipe chambers in the original architectural plan. During that time, the necessary equipment had been promised from a church in the city of St. Louis. However, that church began to experience a renewed growth and decided to keep its organ.

107 Humberg, William M. *The Lloyd Daugherty Memorial Organ.* (Dardenne Presbyterian Church, Dardenne Prairie, MO. 1997) p. 1.

Jerry Leigh was chosen to chair the organ-building project. After finding that a new fully equipped pipe organ was not affordable, the committee determined that the church could build an organ. The project was approved by Session in June and by the following month the first 33 ranks of pipes had been donated.

An assortment of parts that had been squirreled away in office buildings and sheds came to light after more than one hundred years. Pipes, blowers, and consoles began to arrive as the project got underway. Many of the parts dated back to 1888. As the volunteers worked, other parts began to surface in unusual ways. Three U-Haul trailers were rented for a trip to Peoria, Illinois, where old organ parts were to be retrieved.[108] A blower and two ranks of pipes were suddenly "found" in an old barn in Union, Missouri. Word was received that more pipes had been found. A disastrous fire swept through Our Lady of Perpetual Help Catholic Church destroying everything except the pipe organ. The day before it was to be demolished, volunteers rescued 33 ranks of pipes from the old church. A real estate agent in Granite City, Illinois just happened across air regulators and a voicing machine, among other parts, in a real estate deal. In the end, the project united Christians from four states and Canada.

Soon, words like wind chests, shutter motors and Treu and Pheffer began to pepper the volunteers' conversations. Trade-offs began when an organ builder needed some tracker organ parts. Dardenne had them. The builder, in turn, offered a spare wind chest that just "happened" to be the right size for a rank of Dardenne pipes. Day crews and night crews were set up as volunteers, of all ages, began the painstaking work of sorting and straightening pipes. Straightening pipes, as explained by one volunteer, was unique. "By slipping a beat-up old pipe over an arbor (a solid steel bar) and tapping it with a short length of two-by-four, the pipe gradually could be straightened and returned to its original round condition." Sleeves for some of the pipes were made from roof flashing and soda cans. In the end, the ten-ton wonder would have the same cubic space of a three-bedroom ranch home. The real marvel of this story is the fact that none of the part-time volunteer laborers had ever worked on anything like this project before and throughout the entire project, there were no written plans.

As word of the endeavor spread through the community, residents who were not members of the church began to arrive and assist with the painstaking job of renovation. Some stayed after the project was complete to become Dardenne family members.

Several months after the project began; an "Open House" was held in May of 1996. Those not involved in the project were given a once in a lifetime opportunity

---

108 Melton, J. Bruce. *An Organ Transplant or The Body of Christ Gets a New Musical Heart.* (Dr. J. Bruce Melton, St. Charles County, MO. 1998) p. 2

to view the making of an organ system. With project volunteers on hand to answer questions the exhibit was an impressive display of time and talent.

While most materials were donated, the cost to the church was about $100,000. However, the estimated worth of the system is placed at more than $750,000. Twice the size of the original plan, the Lloyd Daugherty Memorial Organ is one of the largest of its kind in the Midwest. It is also twice the size of the famous Fox Theater organ. What began as a variety of parts ready for the junk heap has been converted into a ten-ton musical delight.

In November 1997, only two years after the beginning of the project, the final stage was completed when the Festival Trumpets were suspended from the ceiling of the nave. Because of their futuristic shape, somewhat reminiscent of the Star Trek Enterprise, members dubbed the pipes "Starship Dardenne". The first time they blasted out with joyous notes during a worship service, Rev. Myers with his ever-present sense of humor, mentioned that he hoped they weren't aimed toward the pulpit.

Ask any of the 100 volunteers how they became involved in the project and they usually smile, shake their heads and say they aren't really sure. Yet, it's evident they not only have fond memories of the time spent but also speak of their work with pride. Hu Weikart, one of the volunteers remembered, "Like many who get involved with church projects, I don't remember how this one began. However, in all my years in church work it was...the most challenging, most involved, most fun and definitely the most fulfilling project."[109]

Dr. J. Bruce Melton, a Dardenne member and volunteer organ maker noted, "The best part of this whole adventurous project is that the interest, skills, and hard work of music-loving Presbyterians is coming to focus across many years and miles. For the next century, one man's love for his fine instrument will be perpetuated in songs of praise to God from another congregation of fellow-Christians."[110]

109 Weikart, Hubert. Correspondence to Diane Rodrique—March, 17, 2002.
110 Melton, Dr. J. Bruce. *An Organ Transplant or The Body of Christ Gets A New Heart* (Dr. J. Bruce Melton, St. Charles County, 1998) p. 2.

Chapter 8

Welcome To the Family

September of 1996 brought yet another historical milestone to Dardenne. In its 177-year history, Dardenne had known only four installed pastors. On September 8, 1996, Rev. Gary Myers was installed as its first co-pastor. In 1973, Rev. Myers was Associate Pastor of Bonhomme Presbyterian Church and was appointed by the Presbytery to moderate the Pastoral Nominating Committee that sought a pastor for Dardenne after the passing of Rev. Bunce. It was that Committee that called Rev. Sale to Dardenne. Now, 23 years later, as Rev. Sale looked toward retirement, Rev. Myers returned from a long and successful pastorate in Bartlesville, Oklahoma and accepted the call to share the Dardenne responsibilities as co-pastor.

A little more than a year after Rev. Myers' arrival, another segment of Dardenne history came to a close. In December 1997 Rev. Thomas Sale retired. He had faithfully ministered to the needs of Dardenne for twenty-three years and had seen tremendous change during that time. Upon his arrival in 1974, the 186 members worshipped in the Rock Church. When he retired, Dardenne was over 1,000 members strong. During his tenure he and the congregation implemented the renovation of Watson Hall, the building of Salmon and Robinson Halls and the completion of the Brick Church. Dardenne will always be grateful to Rev.

Sale for his dedication, foresight and leadership. His countless accomplishments saw an emerging country church grow to become a regional leader.

A Kansas City native, "Pastor Gary" graduated from Central Missouri State University in 1962 and Princeton Theological Seminary in 1965. Internships were at New Lebanon, Missouri and Church of the Covenant in Wilmington, Delaware. After ordination, he served in Gladstone and Stony Point churches near Kansas City before serving 14 years at Bonhomme Presbyterian Church. After 13 years as pastor of First Presbyterian Church of Bartlesville, he was called to Dardenne. He and his wife, Jean, have four sons and two grandchildren living in the Kansas City and Oklahoma areas.

Reverend Gary Myers
First Co-Pastor—1997. Fifth Installed Pastor—1998

In June of 2002, Pastor Gary wrote: "It is the end of June 2002, and Jean and I have been at Dardenne for six years. Looking back over this time, I see a number of blessings which have been part of our life here in this wonderful congregation. God has been evident in the life and witness of this Church in ways that amaze me. I see a blessing in the wonderful support of prayer from so many in the congregation. This has been magnified in those times when members have gathered around me for prayer or supported special prayer services in the nave."

"Another blessing has been the responsive way in which the congregation has grown in its singing praise to God in worship. It means so much to me to see people praising and adoring our Lord in services on Sunday and other times."

"The growth of the Mission Budget, which has doubled over these years, as well as the reaching out of the community in service through HOPE, Habitat for Humanity, and Mentoring, and in other ways warms my heart."

"To work with the Session and the Staff of the Church has touched me deeply, especially at times when we have had to make difficult decisions, to risk moving ahead in new ministries, and to expand our horizons. All of this makes me know that God is leading us in exciting ways and the future that the Lord has for us will be both challenging and rewarding. Glory to God!"[111]

Pastor Gary demonstrates his love of the Lord and dedication to His work as he applies his determined, focused and caring leadership in meeting the tough challenges of a growing 21st Century church. With the tragic events of September 11, 2001, his love and strength acted as a beacon of light and hope to the congregation during the dark days following the terrorist attacks. After those events, a newspaper article from Rev. Myers reminded area readers, "In most cases, the fanatic's God is spiteful, domineering and inflexible—a God of vengeance always ready to condemn. We were reminded that, as Christians, we have a God of Love always ready to forgive. We can condemn fanatics while also embracing the wiser course of enthusiasm (which comes from 'en theos' or 'in God.'")

August of 1998 brought Associate Pastor Lewis C. Kimmel and his family to Dardenne. Rev. Kimmel grew up in Asheville, North Carolina and graduated high school in suburban Washington, D.C. He joined the US Marine Corps and served in Vietnam from 1966-1970. He recognized the Lordship of Jesus Christ in June 1971. He graduated from Wake Forest University in 1974. In 1984, he graduated Columbia Theological Seminary and married Jennie Langham. He has served as United States Navy Chaplain from 1984-1993 and the PCUSA Church in the Charlotte, North Carolina Presbytery from 1993-1998.[112]

---

111 Myers, Rev. Gary correspondence to Diane Rodrique. Dardenne Prairie, MO. 2002.
112 Dardenne Presbyterian website. Rev. Lewis C. Kimmel. (Dardenne Presbyterian Church, Dardenne Prairie, MO. 2002)

Reverend Lewis Kimmel
Associate Pastor—1998

His wife, Jennie, grew up in the mission field and served as a volunteer in Zaire, Africa.

Their devoted efforts with the children and young people have been a blessing to the church. As liaison for the Strengthening Committee, Rev. Kimmel has been involved with numerous youth projects, in addition to continued support of the Sale Library. While his responsibilities to the church require much time, it is evident that he is a devoted family man. During one Sunday service, he took a moment from the usual worship schedule to praise God for the love of his wife, Jennie, and eighteen wonderful years of marriage.

When asked to share his thoughts on his time at Dardenne he replied, "My introduction to Dardenne came when someone called and…my recollection is that they said, "We are a little church in Dardenne Prairie, Missouri and are interviewing candidates for Associate Pastor. Now...I graduated from high school in the Washington, D.C. area...and spent other years on the East Coast and in the South. I had no interest whatsoever in heading inland....especially to the Midwest and certainly I was not interested in serving a church on the Dardenne *Prairie*."

"It's amazing how our desires can be so easily changed when we sense the tug of the hug of Jesus. Upon getting to know those who were tasked with seeking an Associate Pastor, Jennie and I sensed very soon in the process...the deep, deep commitment of Dardenne to the telling of and living out the teachings of Jesus Christ. I have witnessed here as much grace and trust and love and JOY as any fellowship I have encountered in the world. There is no question that God has his hand upon this congregation, and is in the process of maturing us, equipping us, blessing us and commissioning us to share with others that He is who He says He is!"

"I am very appreciative of serving Christ among a whole lot of folks who know they are not perfect, yet want to grow in their ability to please God."[113]

About the time that Rev. Myers arrived Dardenne sent its Parish Associate, Rev. Dr. Robert Falconer, to help the struggling fellowship of St. Andrews in Warrenton. Although formed thirteen years before, and in a different Presbytery, Dardenne applied efforts to help the small group establish a Presbyterian church in their area. The group of about 25 regulars and 10 others struggled to continue the fellowship which was never recognized as a church within their Presbytery. When Rev. Falconer retired in November of 1998, the fellowship continued to meet and finally gave up their building. They met for a brief time at the Children's Evangelistic Fellowship until they disbanded in 1999.

Dardenne has made tremendous strides from nine pioneers meeting in the back of a general store on the prairie. Today, Dardenne Presbyterian Church is a regional leader with close to 1,600 members and numerous ministries, both local and foreign.

A 'User-friendly' church

One reason for the church's longevity is the sense of family. Whether a visitor is greeted by a member on the parking lot, the greeters inside the front door, or by one of the ushers, the message is the same: "Welcome." Visitors are often surprised to receive a warm reception upon arrival at a "Big Church". Whether they stay for the service or stay for a lifetime, they discover members are glad to meet and greet new faces. One Dardenne member—Joan Taylor—explained her attraction to Dardenne as follows: "I like the mix of traditional and new music. It's a 'user-friendly' church. There is a lot of work to be done for God and I sense it is a fertile field."

---

113 Kimmel, Rev. Lewis C. Correspondence with Diane Rodrique, June 14, 2002. (Dardenne Presbyterian Church, Dardenne Prairie, MO. 2002).

The ambiance of a typical Sunday morning at Dardenne reminds one of a family gathering. This is evident especially when Rev. Gary Myers or Rev. Lew Kimball stop to visit with members before the service. Among Dardenne family members they are affectionately known as Pastor Gary and Pastor Lew. Just prior to any one of the three services, Sunday School or junior church service, members gather to visit, share a happening of the past week, or check on any number of special projects being offered by different groups, committees or ministries. Usually those visitors who enter the first time with a preconceived notion that a "Big" church isn't friendly, soon find that the Dardenne family offers a loving and caring atmosphere for each member. Dardenne is a family church of brothers and sisters joining together to worship God and make His message known to others. Each gathering, whether on Sunday morning or during the week, the message is clear: Each day is a joyous event to be celebrated.

A walk through Watson, Salmon or Robinson Hall reveals how Dardenne is an active, vital, church. An inquiry class for new members meets in the parlor. Close to the library and the nursery, shopping carts are lined up to receive donations for current mission projects, of which there are usually several. Any number of activity announcements line the tables. The choice is as varied as the imagination allows. Downstairs, in Watson Hall and on the second floor of the Christian Life Center, Sunday School classes meet for age groups from youngsters to senior citizens.

On Sunday mornings, between services, members gather in Mission Hall for doughnuts and coffee and a moment to visit with each other. Some members, who belong to more than one activity in the church, find it is the ideal time to catch up on the latest news about a group activity. Usually many groups use the time between services to offer an opportunity to buy tickets for a baseball outing, voter registration, a Red Cross drive or collect peanut butter or coffee for one of many mission projects.

What began as a charter for a Sunday School Class in 1830 has now grown to include, adults, children, and a Junior Church. Currently nine Adult classes provide for any interest in enhancing spiritual life; including one class organized for singles. An annual Vacation Bible School during one week of the summer developed as a result of the Sunday School classes. During June of 2002 the Vacation Bible School attracted 298 youngsters for a joyous week of activities designed to teach children more about God. By 2004, the church prepared 100 helpers for a projected 500 children to attend the Vacation Bible School.

In 1819, Dardenne Presbyterian began as a mission church and the staff consisted of one part-time Stated Supply Pastor and no building. Originally, members met in members' homes or in John Naylor's General Store. Through the years we have worshipped in a general store, members' homes, a log cabin, a small church, a brush arbor, a rock church and the magnificent structure we have today. In 2004,

Dardenne is blessed with a complex of buildings, a 15-member staff and a generous, talented and accomplished congregation.

We know that God calls each of His children to a particular task just as the Scots/Irish settlers were blessed with His call to Dardenne Prairie. Their rich, powerful history strengthened their faith and firmly established a love of stewardship needed to build that first log cabin church at Dardenne Creek. Through the years, Dardenne has grown, faltered, and grown again. But not once, through all that time, have we lost sight of our dedication to His work. Now that Dardenne has entered the twenty-first century we are even more committed to the belief that we are each called to use our unique gifts and talents for the glory of God. May we always be blessed with His love.

The Christian Life Center was dedicated June 30, 2002. The 30 X 50 foot stage is approximately the size of the brick Dardenne Presbyterian Church which was destroyed by fire during the Civil War. The CLC auditorium has a seating capacity of 900 persons.

Chapter 9

The New Millennium

A Letter to Rev. Billy Graham

In 1962, when our church had reached, perhaps, its lowest point, we were on the brink of losing a bequest left to us by Earle Tyler Castlio. Her final request had been to bequeath $10,000 to the church if we could meet the stipulations of her Will. However, we could not meet the request. In an effort to stave off the loss, Rev. Stuart Salmon wrote a touching letter to Rev. Billy Graham. If we did not meet the stipulations of the Castlio will, the Billy Graham Foundation and the Children's Evangelical Foundation (CEF) would divide the Dardenne portion of the bequest. As a small country church we were struggling to survive. The local court ruled against Dardenne, then the Missouri Supreme Court ruled against our church and the money was awarded to Graham's Foundation and the CEF. On the surface, it seemed a loss, however, some miracles seem just that at first. The event became a catalyst for renewed and unprecedented growth at Dardenne. When Rev. Salmon's letter came to light, in 2002, the Session sent another letter to Rev. Graham. This time, we reported the joyous news of what had happened to our church during the forty-year interim. Both letters are printed in their entirety and are set to match the font used in this book.

December 20, 1962
The Rev. Dr. Billy Graham
Montreat, North Carolina
Dear Sir and Brother:

Having many times listened and watched while you preached on television and the radio, and having had one cherished occasion of hearing you preach at Montreat and of sharing in a long afternoon consultation with you and several score of other ministers there, I believe I know something of your spirit and heart. I cannot, therefore, really believe that you are aware of and willingly a party to a suit nearing trial in the Circuit Court of St. Charles County, just across the Missouri River. This letter is only to you personally, sent to you at your home address, and registered for delivery to you, for your information.

Mrs. Earle Graves Tyler Castlio left her entire estate to her brother, who died before her as it turned out. The residuary legatees were three in number, to share equally. They are: The Billy Graham Foundation, the Child Evangelism Fellowship, and her own church, Dardenne Presbyterian Church. However, there was a stipulation that within nine months of the day of her death the Church "have a full-time pastor holding regular services" or words to that effect. It was clear to the Probate Court that the first phase she meant an ordained minister rather than a layman, since services had frequently been held by laymen and she had manifested dissatisfaction with this as a regular arrangement and knew that no resident pastor was conceivably possible. The court also adjudged the second phrase rightly interpreted by determination of what was "regular" in this particular instance since the schedule of various churches vary almost infinitely. On both counts, the Probate Court ruled in the Church's favor, and therefore the Church was to share with the other two. Many old friends are prepared to testify that this church was the one institution most dear to her heart, and which she said "must be kept going for the sake of the youth to come after us."

But now, not content with a windfall inheritance of some $10,000 each, the other two legatees have appealed the case, and it is scheduled for trial January 5.

Regular services, always by ordained ministers, under the specific direction of the Presbytery's Church Extension Committee by order of the Presbytery itself, have been held for the last eight months, and are definitely and determinedly fixed for the future. Another Ruling Elder is to be elected in a Congregational Meeting following the service on December 30. Four new members were received at our service on November 25. The future is bright with promise, since several very large housing developments are in various stages of planning, development, and even sales already, in the close vicinity, and this church has Comity rights in this area.

And may I take this opportunity to express my sincere thanks and appreciation for all you are doing for the Kingdom, as you have gladly been used of the Holy Spirit throughout the world. May God's richest blessing abide with you and yours, not only in the Christmas and New Year season, but always and all ways.

Yours in His service,
S. H. Salmon

Forty years later: A Letter of Joy

Dr. Billy Graham
BGEA, P.O. Box 779
Minneapolis, MN 55440
April 20, 2002
RE: Strife on Dardenne Prairie, Missouri 1962
Dear Dr. Graham;

Our History Task Force is in the process of preparing our church's 183-year history for publication later this year. We were a pioneer church founded by a missionary pastor in 1819 and counted some of Daniel Boones survey party in our first membership. In our research certain information has been uncovered which closely links Dardenne Presbyterian Church with the Billy Graham Foundation.

We attach Dr. Salmon's letter, our Stated Supply Pastor, addressed to you and dated December 20, 1962, and a copy of the Missouri Supreme Court's ruling on this struggle between our two organizations. This 1960's information is not disputed and fairly represents the desperate situation of our deteriorating congregation.

At our church's monthly Session meeting April 16, 2002, the Elders discussed the various ways this chapter should be closed and forever put behind us. As you can imagine some older members who survived the incident have thought long and hard about it and have come gently to this conclusion. We have elected to write a letter to you and others who also survive and may indeed wonder what became of the Dardenne Presbyterian Church, USA, the little church on the prairie?

We bring good news! We survived, filled with Christian love, inspired, robust and growing. We have 1,400 members and we are completing a new Christian Life Center with seating for 900. We are blessed with a dedicated, devoted and a generous congregation who are vitally involved in the community. When the Billy Graham 2000 Revival came to St. Louis, Missouri, Dardenne Presbyterian Church sent busloads of local folks 40 miles every night to worship and praise God with you. Thirty choir members and 10 of our members were counselors with people on the floor of the TWA Dome. What a week! Now our Youth

Ministry E-Team has been selected as one of the ten teams to participate in Evangelism training at Billy Graham Cove Training Camp and we are sending a leader and four youth. Dr. Salmon's 1960's prediction of vital service to the area's youth was indeed visionary.

We believe it is important for you to know, we now believe our disappointment in 1962 became a wake-up call and a baptism of fire. Our trials stiffened our resolve and steeled our battle to survive. Yes, as Presbyterians we might even say "Predestined" to overcome our adversities. Our Father in heaven works in wondrous ways! Who could have ever predicted this outcome from such a divisive issue between our two organizations.

After reading this letter we prayerfully request that an ambassador from your organization participate in our first Mission Conference at our church this fall, October 13-16, 2002. For you see, we are now poised to go out into the entire world as a mission-focused church. Now, the Billy Graham Foundation and Dardenne Presbyterian Church can boast of our strength being linked together forever in His Name! Please help us write this new chapter in our church history replacing the old "…Success always lies in the future not in the past.*

In His Service,

Dorothy Morgan, Clerk of the Session

P.S. Oh yes, by the way, we are meeting every Sunday nowadays! In fact, Easter 2002 we had four services in one day compared to the early 1960's when we struggled to have four in one year.

* Quoted from Rev. Thomas L. Sale, Retired Senior Pastor Dardenne Presbyterian Church.

The Christian Life Center

June of 2000 brought the start of another building phase to Dardenne. Long-time church members, Jim Mouser, and Don Pettig were chosen to co-chair the Building Council for the $3.1 million dollar Christian Life Center. Groundbreaking for the new building was held in April 2001 with a ceremony immediately following Sunday's 11 a.m. service. In the best Scots tradition, a bagpiper participated in the service, and led the congregation directly from the nave to the groundbreaking site.

The fund-raising campaign, "Our Vision for God's Glory" produced immediate results with gifts and financial commitments. By the first anniversary of the campaign kick-off, church members held a gathering to celebrate the campaign's progress. Donations and pledges by church members had reached one-third of the amount needed. Initially, the Sunday School classes, as part of their Sunday School Outreach program, had given a three-year pledge. The children demonstrated their enthusiasm for the new building, which would house many of their activities including Vacation Bible School, by raising their entire pledge within the first year of the project. Since then they have decided to double their original pledge amount.

Just fifteen months after groundbreaking, the new building was dedicated on June 30, 2002. Using the theme, "Touching Tomorrow Together," the dedication program included the placement of the cornerstone, and a bronze Giving Tree in the foyer. The time capsule, situated behind a brass plate at the main entrance of the building, contains memorabilia pertinent to Dardenne in 2002.[114] All church members were encouraged to contribute something memorable to share with future Dardenne generations. The celebration was typical of a Dardenne gathering with worship music, good fellowship, laughter, and great food. The Fellowship Players, Dardenne's histrionic artists, offered their version of the popular reality show, Survivor.

One of the most touching moments in a day filled with historical significance was the brief, but emotionally stirring, commissioning of Marc R. Sikma as Dardenne's Youth Minister. In his brief remarks to the crowd he noted that, "I cannot describe my excitement in being your new Youth Minister. Here at Dardenne, we have a tremendous youth group—both middle school and high school. We also have a great parent leadership, a loving church, a superb facility and a caring God who brings it all together for His glory! I ask for your prayers as we begin this journey together."

The Time Capsule

After the Christian Life Center cornerstone was sealed in a special dedication ceremony, the Dardenne Time Capsule was sealed. The time capsule was placed indoors at the main entrance (Highway N) of the Christian Life Center behind a brass dedication plaque. According to Hu Weikart, Commitment Committee Elder and Chair of the History Task Force, the information was assembled by the History Task Force. Its purpose was to provide some insight into the prayers, hopes and dreams of the congregation at that time. The church plans to open the time capsule at the time of Dardenne's 200th anniversary celebration, September 18, 2019.

---

114 Weikart, Hubert Closing of Time Capsule Program, Dardenne Presbyterian Church, Dardenne Prairie, Missouri. June 30, 2002.

The Giving Tree

A copper tree with individual engraved brass leaves graces the wall at the Highway N entrance of the Christian Life Center. It was dedicated by Clyde and Jim Mouser and allows church members to give gifts of $300 or more in memory of, or in honor of, an individual accomplishment—or simply to honor God. The tree is a gift to the church from family and friends of Hugo Brown and Bob Stegeman. It was dedicated to the Glory of God the same day the Christian Life Center was blessed.

The Thomas Sale Library

In June of 2002, the church library received a new home. The room that had formerly housed the nursery, was renovated for library use. The expanded quarters were designed by then-Librarian Barbara Buchanan while new shelving and cabinetry were provided by craftsmen Chuck and Judy Poe. Mrs. Buchanan began the process of bringing the library into the computer age and Internet accessibility. Through diligent efforts over several decades and the faithful support of church members, the library has known steady growth.

On the same day the new Christian Life Center was dedicated, the church library was dedicated as the Rev. Thomas L. Sale Library. Mr. Jim Mouser, Facilities Manager, led the call to worship and Rev. Lew Kimmel led the prayer of dedication. Upon their arrival to the church, Rev. Tom Sale (1974), Rev. Gary Myers (1996) and Rev. Lew Kimmel (1998) had all encouraged the growth and development of the church library project. It was during the time that the library was housed in the conference room next to the staff office that an "Open Door Policy" and "Honor System" was initiated. It is an "Honor System" which continues to this day. Just as Dardenne has known only five installed pastors in its entire history, the church library has known just six librarians. Sue Spellman (1972), Madelyn Hopper (1974), Iona Humberg (1995), Audrey Kraemer-Duff (2000), the late Barbara Buchanan (2000) and Doris Liesman (2003).

What began as "a few books and the Vacation Bible School Curriculum" has now grown to about 3,300 volumes, including an extensive reference and video and audiotape section—with more arriving every day. Taped copies of the weekly worship service and special events are also housed in the library and are available for viewing. The children's section has been set aside in one area of the library to accommodate younger members of the church and includes an excellent collection of books and videos.

The Mission Conferences

In May of 1969, as Dardenne was struggling to make a comeback, the one-page Dardennaire newsletter noted, "We look forward to the day when Dardenne can materially assist other churches and give generous support to missionary and other benevolence." That day came on October 13, 2002, when Dardenne came full circle from a mission church created in a general store to holding its first Mission Conference in the newly opened Christian Life Center.

It seemed appropriate that a tiny mission church should grow to dedicate itself to mission work. The mission conference takes over a year of careful planning by a Mission Committee team. A year of weekly meetings and dedicated work brings together missionaries from around the world who offer a variety of opportunities for service to God. Whether a person wants to work with local groups or become involved in foreign mission work, expert guidance is available from experienced professionals at the conferences.

From the beginning, the Mission Conferences were successful measured by the volunteer response of the attendees. Although the first conference did not have a representative of the Billy Graham Evangelical Association, as requested by our Session, the conference showed that Dardenne members were ready to open their hearts and offer their services to a variety of mission projects.

From the opening procession into the nave, and sermon by missionary Harold Kurtz, to the closing prayer at the Wednesday morning breakfast, three days later, the first Dardenne Mission Conference was well attended. With twenty-nine missionaries to share their stories, their hopes and dreams, and a myriad of exhibits, the Holy Spirit was at work. Throughout the Conference, there were workshops, panel discussions, praise and worship. One evening was set aside for dinner with the missionaries in members homes. It was an opportunity to break bread and get to know the people who dedicated their lives to mission field work.

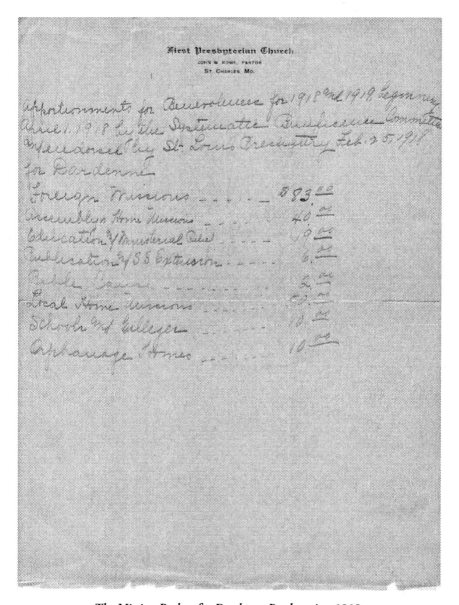

The Mission Budget for Dardenne Presbyterian 1918.
The handwritten message is thought to be that of Rev. Samuel McCluer Watson

A well-rounded four-day program included:

- Harold Kurtz-Presbyterian Frontier Fellowship-Keynote speaker
- Janet Snyder and Trevor Brown-Child Evangelism Fellowship
- David Robinson-Campus Crusade for Christ
- Fernando Hernandez-Bridge Ministry
- Homas Zafer-Barnes Jewish Hospital
- Jimmie Rivera-Mission Discovery
- Jeff Woodke-Sudan Inland Mission and Youth With A Mission
- Jerry Chappeau-City Lights Mission
- Terry and Lorie Lingel International Gospel Ministries
- Rich and Lynn Norton-Mission to the World
- Carl and Carol Vorst-House of Hope
- James Gleaves-New Tribes Mission
- Ken and Martha Shirkey-U.S. Center for World Missions
- Aimee Wiggers-Bethany Christian Services
- Brent and Connie Gregory Project Amazon
- Heather Steen—Global Mapping International
- Jim and Brenda Van Winkle
- Gary and Shirley Wade-World Indigenous Missions
- Dave and Linda Zarro-World Mission Video

David Robinson, Harold Kurtz and friends in prayer on the final day of the Mission Conference 2002.
Photo courtesy of Rick Sabbert

The final day of the conference found many gathered at a local restaurant for an early morning breakfast and the opportunity to hear David Robinson speak about his service to the Lord with Campus Crusade for Christ.

But, the real story came to light in the coming weeks and months, as the numbers of volunteers increased in both local and foreign mission work. In some cases, volunteer numbers doubled—especially among Tide members! Talking to the members, it is evident that Dardenne is a church dedicated to sharing the gospel with the world.

Subsequently, the second Mission Conference held in October 2003 was just as successful and included Gary Haugan, President and CEO of the International Justice Mission as the keynote speaker. The Steve Green concert, on Monday evening, played to standing room capacity. Once again, various booths from mission organizations lined the Christian Life Center and Mission Hall.

Four days of meetings, breakfasts, breakout sessions, prayer and praise were heavily attended by enthusiastic participants. Question and Answer "Interview Panels" were led by Mary Ellen Lopez and Marvin Cave. Dinners in private homes with the missionaries were all a part of the opportunity for the Conference attendees to learn more about mission work. The second conference closed on Wednesday, October 15th with speaker Gustavo Crocker of World Relief. While some of the presenters from the first conference returned, new organizations also were present for the second conference:

- ◆ James Gleason-New Tribes Mission
- ◆ Brian Gregory-Project Amazon
- ◆ Brian Hart-Intervarsity Christian Fellowship
- ◆ Gary Haugen-International Justice Mission
- ◆ Fernando Hernandez and Gary Liebovich-New City Fellowship
- ◆ Ralph Hord-Literacy and Evangelism International
- ◆ Gilbert Jules-Ambassadors for Christ in Haiti
- ◆ Solomon Kendogar-International Student Inc.
- ◆ Caroline Kurtz-Presbyterian Frontier Fellowship
- ◆ C.J. Guinness-International Justice Mission
- ◆ Carolyn Newcomb-Join Hands Against Hunger
- ◆ Jim Romaine-Zwemer Institute
- ◆ Lynne Swinke-Workman-Medical Benevolence Foundation
- ◆ Mel West-Personal Energy Transportation

Chapter 10

Footsteps of Devotion:
The Dardenne Histories

Throughout Dardenne history, the women of the congregation have kept records of the stories and events of the church. Within the last year, three gems have been found within the treasure of the Dardenne archives. Old, and long-forgotten manuscripts that had been stapled behind other articles and filed away in vinyl binders, have been brought to light. Suddenly finding such a large amount of valuable information brings home the message that all things are revealed in God's time.

The following histories have been recorded here in an effort to save the fading original manuscripts. However, spelling and accuracy, as they appeared in the original manuscripts have remained intact. Any inaccuracies are those of the original historian. In the re-telling of events from one historian to the next, one finds that certain episodes are presented in a different light by each historian. Philosophically the issue could be debated on the numerous reasons for such an occurrence, however, we may assume that all the histories are presented with the same thought, i.e., to record the events, struggles, and celebrations of the Dardenne family who relied on their faith in God under all circumstances.

The Dardenne Presbyterian Church: A Brief History

Mrs. William C. Wilson-1944. (This history was written for a booklet published for Dardenne's 125th Anniversary.)

> *Dardenne Presbyterian Church was established September 18, 1819 as part of the missionary effort of the Rev. Charles S. Robinson, pastor of the First Presbyterian Church, St. Charles, Missouri. He had been sent to the Territory as a Missionary by the Young Men's Missionary Society of New York.*
>
> *Early meetings of the Scotch-Irish congregation, beginning with eight founding members, were held in the homes of member's; later a log church was built near Dardenne Creek. The name "Dardenne" is also shared with Dardenne Township in which the church is located and with Dardenne Prairie, the fertile farmlands settled in the early 1800's by pioneers across the Mississippi River.*
>
> *The present stone edifice was erected in 1868, a few years after the earlier permanent structure of brick on the original site, was burned during the War Between the States by "parties unknown". The church is located on the Boone's Lick Road, a route laid out by Daniel Boone during his late years as a citizen of this region of Missouri.*
>
> *Through its long life Dardenne Church has been served by only two installed pastors; The Rev. Thomas Watson, who was pastor from 1844, following his graduation from Princeton Seminary, until just before his death in 1888; and by his son, the Rev. Samuel M. Watson, pastor from 1889 until his passing in 1925. As members of the congregation moved from the community Dardenne Church became less active and served by supply pastors. The recent reactivation of Dardenne Church was begun in 1962 and has been given substantial financial support by the Central Presbyterian Church of Clayton, Missouri, The Presbytery of St. Louis and the General Assembly, U.S.*

The next manuscript by Mrs. Jane Elzea is enlightening. She notes several events which were almost lost to us or were misinterpreted through the years. In the Helen Stewart History dated 1970 and signed in 1971, she observes that the history is taken from the "History of Dardenne Church 1819-1944" by Mrs. William C. Wilson. Wilson's source, it's noted, came from the Session books of the church. The original manuscripts, typewritten and mimeographed, have faded during the course of time. However, every effort has been made to adhere to the original wording and format. For space purposes, the original page headings as noted on page 2 were deleted. Mrs. Stewart, in an effort to preserve our history, goes one step further by including information from church services. It's interesting to note how our Sunday worship service has changed over the years.

Mrs. Stewart, Mrs. Wilson and Mrs. Elzea have preserved the story of a very unique time in our history, one of struggle, growth and renewal. Some reason it was a time that, until now, was thought to be saved only in the memory of those who lived it. We are indebted to them for their exacting records which brings to light some facts long obscured. Events of special interest have been placed in bold type. Additionally, the information provided on the creation and activities of the Presbyteens provides insight to the activities of those young adults in the late 1960's and 1970's.

HISTORY OF DARDENNE CHURCH
COMPILED BY MRS. JANE ELZEA
COPIED BY MRS. HELEN STEWART

Dardenne Church was organized September 18, 1819, at the home of Mr. John Naylor, in Dardenne Township, St. Charles, County Missouri by Rev. Charles S. Robinson the pastor of the First Presbyterian church, St. Charles, Missouri, as a part of his Missionary work. For which he was sent out, by the Young Men's Missionary Society of New York.

The following were Charter Members: Mr. & Mrs. John Naylor, and son James Naylor; Mrs. Elizabeth McPheeters; Mr. Adam Zumwalt and his wife Jessie Canton Zumwalt; Mr. Nathaniel Beverly Tucker and his wife Mary.

A log building was erected on land near Dardenne Creek, given by Mr. Adam Zumwalt. This building was later replaced by a brick church.

Dardenne Church was served by supply pastors from its organization in 1819 to 1844. The ministers supplying the pulpit were: Rev. Charles S. Robinson, Rev. William B. Lacy, Rev. John S. Ball, Rev. Warren Nichols, Rev. Hiram Chamberlain, and Rev. R. G. Barrett.

The Elders were: John Naylor, Nathaniel Tucker, George E. Baswell, Dr. Robert McCluer, Lewis Howell, John Castlio, William C. Logan, Cary Allen Boyd, John Adams.

The first recorded meeting of Presbytery to be held at this church was April, 1830 and the last meeting in what is known as "Old Dardenne Church" was September 1858.

At a meeting of Session November 27, 1841 the Moderator, Rev. Robert G. Barrett, stated that Presbytery had directed the Session to dismiss each person that was desirous of being connected with the church soon to be organized at Femme Osage; the Session dismissed: Jonathan Thomas and his wife Amanda Thomas; Issac Darst and his wife Phoebe Darst, Katherine Moore, Nancy G. Taylor, Katherine Stapp as they wanted to unite with the new church.

In November, Session received as members of the church; Eli Lay and his wife Emily Ann Lay; Marcus Lay; Milo Boone and his wife Lucinda Boone; Mrs. Jane McCormich; Mrs. Lucinda Gould; Mrs. Jemima Keller; Mrs. Catherine Moore.

These people had been members of Femme Osage Church, but the church being in a disorganized condition, they with the consent of Presbytery decided to join the church nearest them.

In 1844, Dardenne church called their first pastor, Rev. Thomas Watson, who had been preaching for them the last five months. He had been licensed to preach at a meeting of Presbytery held at Olivet Church, April 12, 1844. He accepted the call and was ordained and installed as pastor November 10, 1844.

During the War between the States, the church building was burned. No one knew who was the perpetrator of the deed. No date of the burning is given, but the last recorded minutes of the Session at the church were dated April 6, 1862. For Several years the congregation worshipped in pleasant weather in "The Arbor", a primitive structure made of posts covered with limbs of trees, or in school houses. Later arrangements were made with the Methodist Congregation at Mechanicsville to use their church building.

On September 18, 1872, Presbytery ordered the membership to be divided. The members living in and near Mechanicsville forming an organization to be known as "South Dardenne". Rev. Thomas Watson continued ministering both congregations. These congregations have been closely allied ever since, but, from this time, each must necessarily have its own history. Though the congregations were divided, they still have their Old Dardenne Cemetery.

In 1868, a new stone building was erected on land bought from Judge and Mrs. Barton Bates, near the center of Dardenne Prairie, on the Old Trail or Boone's Lick Road.

In 1885, Rev. Samuel M. Watson became pastor of the South Dardenne church, Rev. Thomas Watson giving all his time to Dardenne Church until ill health forced him to resign in April 1888 thus ending a pastorate of 44 years. His death occurred June 3, 1888 and his funeral service was conducted by Rev. T.C. Smith, Rev. Robert Brank and Rev. R.P. Farris, members of the Presbytery and his close friends for many years. Dr. Farris, a schoolmate, had been licensed years before. The two congregations united in erecting a fitting monument to the memory of their pastor for so many years. In the months that following the pastor's resignation, Dardenne Church had no regular pastor but was under the care of Rev. T.C. Smith.

In January 1889, Rev. Samuel Watson was invited by the Session to become the stated supply and in November 1892, he was installed pastor of the church;

thus again did South Dardenne and Dardenne come under one pastorate. Rev. R. P. Farris preached the sermon and delivered the charge to the pastor, and Rev. J.E. Latham charged the people.

During the winter of 1901 and 1902 letters of dismissal were granted to 14 or more members to unite with a church to be organized in O'Fallon, Missouri.

Many meetings of Presbytery have been held in the present building between 1868 and 1944. No history of the church would be complete if mention were not made of the good work done in the Sunday School by the superintendents, teachers through the yew years [sic]. One outstanding Bible teacher was Miss Hester Bates, later Mrs. Graves, teacher of the ladies Bible Class. Another, the teacher of the men's class, Mr. Samuel Wilson and the boy's class, Mr. Henry Watson. With many others that might be mentioned. Nor would be complete without mention made of the faithful organist, Mrs. R. G. Woodson, who for many years was in her place at almost every service.

Names of the Elders who have served this church since 1868 are: James Hensell, J.B.Gamble, John Andrew Bailey, William Campbell, Oscar McCluer, James W. Wilson, Thomas Watson Jr. Dr. M.L. Currier, Henry Watson, Ruffner Watson, Curtis Snyder.

Names of Trustees are John W. Wilson, Hilary Ball and Hunter Hutchings. The Deacons were Eugene Muschany, George T. Woodson, Sr., Arthur McCluer, William A. Harris and Louie McCluer.

From this church have gone several Ministers; Rev. Uncas McCluer, Rev. Edwin McCluer, Rev. William C. McCluer, Rev. Samuel Watson, Rev. Herbert H. Watson, Mr. Allen Boyd and Mr. Goodridge B. Wilson as lay preachers.

Rev. Samuel M. Watson served as pastor until he passed away April 9, 1925 at his home in Maplewood, to which place he had moved sometime before, then continuing his pastoral work in his two churches. His funeral was held in South Dardenne by several members of Presbytery. His grave, at his request, is at the Old Dardenne Cemetery. Since his death, a number of Ministers have given part of their time to supplying the pulpit: Rev. Daryl Davis, Rev. Fred Reeves, Rev. L.V. McPherson, Rev. William C. Colby, Rev. Glenn Williams. Rev. Herbert Watson.

Roster of those who attended [sic] the celebration of the 125th Anniversary of Dardenne Church September 24, 1944: William C. Martin, Mrs. William C. Martin, Dr. Frank L. McCluer, Mrs. Frank L. McCluer, Paul Herriott, Mrs. Paul Herriott, John Lynes, Mrs. Martha Jett, Joshua Richmond, Mrs. Joshua Richmond, Herbert H. Watson, Mrs. Herbert H. Watson, Dr. Walter M. Langtry, Mrs. Walter M. Langtry, Tarlton Pittman, Mrs. Tarlton Pittman, Dr. A.D. Willkinson, Mrs. A.D. Willkinson, David Willkinson, Mrs. Cora Stallard

Grave, Miss Anna S. Ball, Ralph K. Watson, Mrs. Ralph K. Watson, P.L. Green, Mrs. P.L. Green, Mrs. Agnes Showers, William A. Langtry, Arthur McCluer, Mrs. Caroline McCluer, Camilla McCluer, Ann McCluer, V.C. McCluer, Mrs. V.C. McCluer, Private Virgil McCluer, George M. Johnson, George M. Johnson, Jr., M.D. Keithly, Mrs. Elroy A. Schweitzer, Elroy A. Schweitzer, Mrs. Martha Kenner, Robert A. Towers, Mrs. Robert A. Towers, Miss Mary Vouga, Miss Stella Alexander, Miss Jennie Alexander, Miss Isabelle Vouga, Erskine Reid, Mrs. Erskine Reid, Miss Mertia Callaway, Tarlton Woodson, Mrs. Tarlton Woodson, Miss Mary Lucille Currier, Miss India Currier, Mrs. J.F. Goellner, J.H. Ball, Mrs. J.H. Ball, Dr. William C. Wilson, Mrs. William C. Wilson, Dr. O.L. Snyder, Mrs. O.L. Snyder, E.H. Zierenberg, Mrs. E.H. Zierenberg, Wanda Lou Zierenberg, Nina Mae Zierenberg, J.E. Fisher, Mrs. J.E. Fisher, Mrs. Henry Hartzog, Mrs. Marcia Williams, Mr. Ben Audrain, Mrs. Ben M. Audrain, John S. Reid, Mrs. John S. Reid, George Calvin Reid, Betty Reid, Martha Jo Reid, Samuel Vouga, Doris Vouga, John Vouga, Larry Vouga, Mrs. Pauline Littman, Mrs. Marguerite Anderson, Mrs. Elizabeth McCluer Calhoon, Mary Calhoon, C.R. Watson, Mrs. C.H. Watson, Mrs. Dina R. Justus, Charley Sidney Johnson, Mrs. Charly Sidney Johnson, Mrs. Margaret Bates Singleton, Mrs. Katherine Singleton Ruthenberg, Mrs. R.L. Fulkerson, Raymond Griesenauer, Mrs. Raymond Griesenauer, William Weyrauch, Mrs. William Weyrauch, W.E. Goodman, E.O. Goodman, Miss Elizabeth P. Goodman, Mrs. Ivan M. Lay, G.C. Pierie, Mrs. G.C. Pierie, Donna E. Pierie, H.A. Hutchings, Elue Diehr, Mrs. George Diehr, Miss Caroline Singleton.

Those that preached at Old Dardenne after the death of S.M. Watson, in 1925, Ministers and Laymen: Dr. Colby, Rev. McPherson, Rev. McCutcheon, Rev. McColgan, Rev. Morton, Dr. Watson, Rev. Williams, Rev. Reeves.

Lay preaching in Dardenne Church and Old Mongomery [sic] School, Ruffner Watson, Curtis Snyder and Mayburn Snyder Ruling Elders.

Some of the South Dardenne Church of Howell, Missouri (Formerly Mechanicsville) moved their membership to Dardenne Church when the T.N.T. took over the area. There were about 10 members.

Mr. Hunter Hutchings and Miss Emily Watson were the only members of Dardenne Church at the time. Some of the members were Charles Ruffner Watson, His wife, Allene, Curtis Snyder and his wife Olive, Mr. and Mrs. P.L. Green, Our first presher [sic] of the Southern Presbyterian Church St. Charles, Missouri. He preached once a month in the afternoon on Sunday beginning in May and ending in October. Mr. McCutcheon followed. Mr. Charles Ruffner Watson became the appointed Lay supply minister until his nervous breakdown.

For several years our Church doors were closed.

In 1962, Church was reopened on April 29th. Dr. S.H. Salmon preached. On the 27th of May there were 31 present.

Mrs. Willie Harris, Agnes Watson, and Mrs. Allene Watson took turns dusting and cleaning the church.

June 24th, 1962 there were 14 people present. July 22 had a good service many old friends and neighbors came. August 15 visiting began, Allene Watson and Willie Harris, August 26th 40 people were present. The collection was $33.95. September 23 about 35 were present. October 28th about 55 were present. November 25, 36 were present, took in 4 new members Miss Sally Watson, Mattie S. Yates, Mr. and Mrs. Melvin Bowman.

Mr. Melvin Bowman was made an Elder February 24, 1963.

Mr. Mayburn Snyder and Mr. Hutchings are Elders also carrying the job of Deacons.

January 1964, 15 were present, Dr. Salmon was preacher.

Mr. Curtis Snyder furnished the first gravel for the parking lot. Mr. Curtis Snyder was elected an Elder for the second time at Dardenne April 26, 1964.

The contract for remodeling the church was to be let on July 15 or 16, 1964.

Mr. and Mrs. Earl Sutton joined the church October 25, 1964.

In 1965 we had church once a month on the fourth Sunday.

March 28, 1965 the old wooden steps and vestibule were torn away.

April 18, 1965 Miss Sally Watson was elected an Elder. May 23, 1965, Sunday Service at 2:30 p.m. Sally Watson and Allene Watson were ordained as Elders.

July 25, 1965 Ray Ferocy, Dr. Salmon's assistant preached for us.

September 26, 1965 services of rededication were held at 2:30 p.m. Extensive renovation of the church has been completed by the committee on church extension of the Presbytery of St. Louis Presbyterian Church in the U.S.

The moderator of the Presbytery, Rev. W. Richard Huey, conducted the service. Gene Barnard, chairman of the church extension committee participated.

Mrs. Melvin Bowman died October 24, 1965. $50 was given by her family for a memorial, 25 hymnals were bought. Mrs. Allene Watson gave the first 15 hymnals.

Mayburn Snyder died January 14, 1966. Dr. Salmon conducted the funeral services.

In May (1966) it was decided to start a Sunday School and church services once a week. Dr. Salmon recommended a young man from the East to be our preacher for three months. Mr. Nick Fenger came and it was decided that on the first and third Sundays of the month, Sunday School would be held at 10 and church services at 11. On the second and fourth Sunday, Sunday School would be held at 1:30 in the afternoon and church services at 2:30. There was very poor attendance.

$124 was given as a memorial fund to Dr. William C. Wilson who had died.

August 28, 1966 Mr. Fenger spoke of leaving the work.

Sunday September 4, 1966, Dr. Herbert Watson preached at 11 o'clock with Sunday School at 10. He was invited by the Session to come to Dardenne to be our preacher. He came and worked very hard visiting in the neighborhood and built the congregation up quite a lot. On October 30, 1966 the Beacham family, husband, wife and three boys were baptized. Mr. and Mrs. Charles Bunce and children joined and the two little children were baptized. Mrs. Jane M. Elzea also joined.

Dr. Herbert Watson drove from his home in Auxvasse, Missouri to do the work of the church. He built the membership up to around 50. The work got to be too much for him, as he had been retired a number of years before he came back to us.

In January 1967 the Sunday School officers were installed: Mr. Clyde Mouser as Superintendent; Mr. James Alexander as assistant Superintendent; Mrs. Helen Stewart as secretary and treasurer.

Mr. Charles Bunce became our pastor when Rev. Herbert Watson had to leave. Mr. Bunce was the religious editor of the Post-Dispatch. St., Louis, Missouri. He is a very qualified man. He was ordained and a pastor of a church in Kentucky. He is hoping to be reordained.

Rev. Watson had a number of Elders and Deacons installed before he left. Mrs. Willie Harris, and Mrs. Allene Watson were made life members of the Deacon Board. Mr. Melvin Bowman and Mr. Curtis Snyder were made life members of the Elders.

Communicant Membership as of November 30, 1969 is 128.

* * * * * * * * * * * * * * * * * *

SOUTHEAST MISSOURI PRESBYTERY
DARDENNE PRESBYTERIAN CHURCH
O'FALLON, MISSOURI 63366
Mrs. Helen Stewart/1970

September 18, 1819:

At a meeting at the home of Mr. John Naylor in the Township of Dardenne, St. Charles County, Missouri, for the purpose of forming by divine permission, a church established on the Presbyterian Discipline, and based on the Scriptures of the Old and New Testament as illustrated by the American Confession of Faith.

The meeting was opened with prayer by Rev. Charles S. Robinson, Mr. John Naylor presented a certificate signed by the Rev. Robert Wilson moderator of the Session of the Presbyterian Church in Washington, Kentucky, testifying that he was a regularly ordained Elder of that church, whereupon it is resolved that he be recognized and received as such in this church.

The following persons on due examination are admitted members of this church: John Naylor, Mrs. John Naylor, his wife, James Naylor, their son, Nathaniel Beverly Tucker, Mrs. Mary Tucker, his wife, Mrs. Elizabeth McPheeters, Adam Zumwalt and Mrs. Zumwalt, his wife.

The meeting was dismissed with prayer.

Signed by order of the meeting,

N.B. Tucker, Clerk, p.t.

(All of the above is quoted directly from the first Session Book of the Dardenne Presbyterian Church.)

I continue with history taken from the "History of Dardenne Church, 1819-1944" compiled by Mrs. William C. Wilson, of St. Charles, Missouri. Mrs. Wilson is still living (as of March 20, 1970). She used the Session books of the church to gather her material.

A log building was erected on land near the Dardenne Creek, which was given by Mr. Adam Zumwalt. (Actually the land was deed by Andrew Zumwalt, brother of Adam Zumwalt). This building, afterwards replaced by a brick building, sat on the top of a wooded hill just across the road from its cemetery—the Old Dardenne Creek Presbyterian Cemetery.

Dardenne Church was served by supply ministers from its organization in 1819 until 1844. There were: Rev. Charles S. Robinson, Rev. William S. lacy; Rev. John S. Ball; Rev. Warren Nichols; Rev. Hiram Chamberlain, Rev. Robert G. Barrett, and Rev. Harliegh Blackwell.

The first recorded meeting of Presbytery held in this church was April, 1830.

In 1844, Dardenne Presbyterian Church called its first full time pastor, Rev. Thomas Watson. He had been licensed to preach at a meeting of Presbytery held at Olivet Church on April 12, 1844. He accepted the call to Dardenne, and was ordained and installed pastor on November 10, 1844.

During the Civil War, this church building was burned. No one knew who was the perpetrator of the deed. No date of the burning is given in the Session Book, but the Last recorded minutes of the Session at the church were dated April 6, 1862. For several years the congregation worshipped, in pleasant weather, in the "Arbor", a primitive structure made of posts covered with limbs of trees, or in school houses. Later arrangements were made with the Methodist Congregation at Mechanicsville (later called Howell), Missouri to use its church building. Session Minutes indicate that the Session, in the meantime, met in the "Arbor," in private homes, in schools or in the Methodist Church mentioned before.

On September 18,1872, Presbytery ordered the membership to be divided. The members living in and near Mechanicsville formed an organization known as "South Dardenne". Rev. Thomas Watson continued to minister to both congregations. Through the years these two congregations were very allied, and they still had, in common, their Old Dardenne Creek Cemetery on the hill.

In 1867 a frame church was built at Mechanicsville, and in 1868 a new stone building was erected by the Dardenne Congregation on land bought from Judge and Mrs. Barton Bates, near the center of Dardenne Prairie, on the Boonslick Road. This building still stands, and is being used by the congregation, and back of it is the new cemetery.

In 1885, Samuel McCluer Watson, son of Rev. Thomas Watson became pastor of South Dardenne Church. Rev. Thomas Watson, then gave all his time to the Dardenne congregation until ill health forced him to resign in April, 1888. In the months following the minister's resignation, the Dardenne Church had no regular pastor, but was under the care of Rev. T.C. Smith.

In January 1889, Rev. Samuel McCluer Watson became stated supply and in November 1892, he was installed pastor of the church; thus again, did Old Dardenne and South Dardenne come under one pastorate. Rev. Samuel McCluer Watson served as pastor until he died on April 9, 1925. His grave, at his request, is at the Old Dardenne Creek Cemetery on the hill. The father and son had a total pastorate of 84 years in the Dardenne and South Dardenne Churches.

Since the death of Rev. Samuel McCluer Watson, there has been no full time minister at the Dardenne Church, but a number of ministers have given part time service in the pulpit; Rev. Daryl Davis, Rev. William S. Colby, Rev, Fred Reeves, Rev. Glen

Williams, Rev. L.V. McPherson, Rev. Herbert H. Watson and Rev. Stuart Salmon. And from July through August 1966, Mr. Nick Fenger was the preacher. While Mr. Fenger was the pastor there were services every Sunday. First and Third Sunday was held in the morning. Second and Fourth Sunday was held in the afternoon. Before that the services were once a month in the afternoon. In 1966 there were 15 members.

In May 1966 a Sunday School was started, only about 10 people attended.

In September, Dr. Herbert H. Watson was invited by the Session to become pastor of Dardenne. He accepted and worked very hard, even though he lived in Auxvasse, Missouri and had already retired from preaching, every Sunday he was here for services. He also came two or three days a week and visited the members.

In January 1967, Mr. Clyde Mouser was installed as Superintendent of the Sunday School; Mr. James Alexander as assistant superintendent; Mrs. Vern Stewart as Secretary and Treasurer; Mrs. James Alexander as pianist and organist, Rev. Dr. Herbert H. Watson served as pastor of Dardenne till May 1967. While he was pastor a very able and consecrated man joined Dardenne. He was the Religion Editor on the Post-Dispatch paper in St Louis, Missouri. The Presbytery appointed Mr. Charles M. Bunce as stated supply pastor.

Shortly after Mr. Bunce took over his duties the Elders and their wives or husbands and the Deacons and their wives or husbands were formed into teams to go on visitation. *Also there was a Junior Choir with Mrs. Martha Alexander as leader. There was a Senior Choir with Mr. Philip Salvati as leader. The youth groups were organized and were named Presbyteens. Women of the Church were organized into two circles. They were very active meeting every month for work, study of the Bible and Fellowship.*

In May 1967, Communion Service, Rev. James Duncan, Pastor of Troy Presbyterian Church in Troy, Missouri and moderator of Dardenne Church administered the Sacrament assisted by Mr. Charles Bunce.

June 1967, the first Vacation Bible School was held for 5 days; Mrs. June Bunce as leader. There were 65 names on the roll, with an average of 59 per day. Twenty-two of those had perfect attendance. There were 17 teachers and helpers.

Junior Choir sang for the first time for morning Worship service on July 23 "He's Got The Whole World In His Hands"

October 1, 1967 World Wide Communion Service was held with Rev. Allen Oakley, Moderator of the Synod of Missouri, and field director for Christian Education, administered the Sacraments.

November, Dardenne held their first Joash Chest Service and Holy Communion with Rev. Herbert H. Watson administering the Sacrament.

Thanksgiving Service was held Wednesday, November 22, 1967 at 7:30 p.m.

A Junior Church was started November 26, 1967 for children 3 years old and up to first grade. The children attend the first part of the Morning Worship Service with their families. When it comes time for the Sermonette they will go down to the front pew with their leaders. Following the Sermonette they and their leaders will go to the trailer for an activity period which lasts until church service is over. The first leaders were Mrs. Opal Comfort; Mrs. Jesse Wilson and Mrs. Owen England.

December 17, 1967, a family fellowship dinner was held at the O'Fallon Community Center, O'Fallon, Missouri. Afterwards, members of both choirs and anyone who wanted to go, went caroling. We sang for shut-ins of our church.

The Christmas Cantata was "A King in the Stable".

January 7, 1968, Holy Communion Service with Rev. Herbert H. Watson administering the Sacrament.

February 4, 1968 a Bible study group for Adults was started, to be held once a month at the homes of Dardenne members and Mr. Donald Pomeroy as leaders.

February 28, 1968, Ash Wednesday Communion Service, Dr. Keith Nickle, Presbyterian theologian on the faculty of St. Louis University Divinity School, administered the Sacrament, assisted by Mr. Charles Bunce, Ordination and installation of Elders and Deacons and reception of new member.

March 10, 1968 a Committee on National Ministries of the Presbytery of St. Louis met at Dardenne at 2 p.m. for an evaluation of the program of the church.

April 7, 1968 Palm Sunday Service, Maundy Thursday Service 8 p.m. Good Friday service at 8 p.m. Easter Service 11 a.m. Maundy Thursday Service Communion Service, Rev. Herbert H. Watson administered the Sacrament.

June 2, 1968, Communion Service was held with Rev. Herbert H. Watson administering the Sacrament.

June 30, 1968 a member of Dardenne Church was the preacher, Mr. Donald Pomeroy. Donald Pomeroy attended Dubuque Presbyterian Seminary and is also a supply minister of the Auburn, Silex and Whiteside churches in Lincoln County, Missouri. Those are the same churches that Mr. Charles Bunce served before he came to Dardenne.

Plans were started to build an Educational Building for Dardenne in July 1968. (Watson Hall)

July 28,1 968 Communion Service and reception of new members with Rev. Herbert H. Watson administering the Sacrament.

August 4, 1968 at 6:30 p.m. Dardenne had its second annual ice-cream social. Members having freezers bringing the ice-cream, other members bringing cake and cookies.

August 18, 1968 Mr. Charles Bunce exchanged pulpits with Dr. Rollyn E. Moseson, pastor of Bonhomme Presbyterian Church, Chesterfield, Missouri. Rev. Moseson succeeded our beloved Dr. Herbert H. Watson at Bonhomme.

Session had charge of the morning Service September 15, 1968. Mr. Charles Bunce was attending a religious journalism seminar at Northwestern University. Guest speaker for Dardenne was an Elder in Des Peres Presbyterian Church, St. Louis County, Missouri. Mr. Eugene Barnard he was also chairman of Presbytery Committee on National Ministries.

October 6, 1968, World Wide Communion with Rev. Robert T. Cuthill, also a reception for new members.

Dardenne's celebration of the 150th anniversary, and the 100th anniversary of the present building began November 22 with a dinner to be served by the ladies of Immaculate Conception Catholic Church, Dardenne, Missouri. The speaker, Dr. Frank H. Caldwell, executive secretary of the Presbyterian Foundation, Charlotte, North Carolina. Dr. Caldwell who is a former Moderator of the General Assembly and President of Louisville Presbyterian Seminary.

Thanksgiving service Wednesday, November 27, 1968 with speaker Rev. Ira Bell, pastor of Immaculate Conception Catholic Church, Dardenne Missouri.

December 1, 1968 at 4:30 p.m. there was an Advent Concert at Dardenne, featuring Mrs. Kathleen Fowler King, Organist at Central Church, Clayton, Missouri. And a vocal ensemble from Central church. This program was a part of Dardenne's anniversary program.

Christmas Cantata "God In A Star". The Christmas Festival Service was Sunday December 22, 1968. Family Vesper Service December 25, at 4:30 p.m. A Watchnight service for youths and Adults was held at 11:30 p.m., December 31, conducted by Mr. Bunce and Mr. Pomeroy.

January 12, 1969, Rev. Raymond A. Schondelmeyer newly appointed director of the Missouri Task Force for Church planning, an agency of Missouri Council of Churches. Formerly pastor of the Presbyterian Church at Steeleville, Missouri. The Rev. Schondelmeyer was also a College and Seminary classmate of Mr. Bunce. He was our preacher.

February 16, 1969 was Preparatory service for Holy Communion.

February 19, 1969, Ash Wednesday, 8 p.m. Rev. L. Vern Trueblood organizing pastor of the Kirk of the Hills Presbyterian Church, St. Louis County, administered the Sacrament.

Holy week services for 1969, Palm Sunday, March 30: Maundy Thursday, April 3; Holy Communion with Rev. Sam Rochester, pastor of Midland Presbyterian Church, St. Louis, Missouri; Easter Sunrise Service (First) 6. a.m. A breakfast was held at 7 a.m. Sunday School at 9:30 a.m.; Morning Worship at 11. New members received at Maundy Service.

May 4, 1969 the choir of the Holy Trinity Serbian Orthodox Church, St. Louis, Missouri, sang a vesper concert at Dardenne church at 4:30 p.m. The Rev. Alexander Dimitrijevich, pastor of Holy Trinity church explained the meaning of some portions of the music. After the concert, we had a family night supper at the VFW Hall in O'Fallon, Missouri with our Serbian friends as guests.

Mr. Hunter Hutchings, an Elder and Trustee-Emeritus and life-long member of Dardenne was found dead at his home May 29, 1969. The funeral was from Pitman's Chapel in Wentzville, Missouri. Mr. Bunce assisted Rev. Roland Boone, pastor of Williams Methodist church in the service. Mr. Hutchings was 75 years old.

May 25, 1969 Pentecost Communion Service was held with Rev. Donald Archibald, Minister of Christian Education at Central Presbyterian Church, Clayton, Missouri, administered the Sacrament, Sermon subject, "When the Holy Spirit Came".

Vacation Church School was held June 9-13 with closing exercises at the Morning Worship Service June 15. A matching set of flags, The Christian and the American, have been presented to the church through two special gifts. The funds for the flags were given by Mr. and Mrs. Aubuchon and their children and by the children of the Vacation Church School.

Dardenne's building plan has been coming along fine. The building fund progressed, for every dollar our church members come up with, Central Presbyterian church of Clayton will match 2-1.

We want to take this opportunity to express our appreciation to Dr. Mauze, Rev. Megahan; Rev. Archibald, the ministers, and the officers and members of Central Church, who have so many times in the past expressed their faith in the program and future of Dardenne, and who continue to do so in such generous and tangible ways. We also appreciate the generosity and interest of Dr. Moseson and the members of Bonhomme Presbyterian Church, Chesterfield, Missouri. We look forward to the day when Dardenne can materially assist other churches, and give generous support to missionary and benevolence causes.

Regarding Service Disruptions: In the event that one of our worship services should receive a visit from Black Militants, or any other group who would disrupt the service. Mr. Bunce has been instructed by the Elders and Deacons to continue the service without interruption, if possible, and if this is not possible, to dismiss the service. The visitors would be invited to remain with us and participate in the

worship if they cared to do so. They would not be allowed to read the Black Manifesto or any other set of demands during the service, but they would be invited to remain after the service and read their statement to any members of the congregation who desire to remain and hear them.

St. Louis Presbytery met at Dardenne church at 4 p.m. Tuesday, June 17, 1969. Of special interest will be the ordination of a Minster at 5:30 p.m. A fellowship dinner at 6 p.m. with the Ministers and Elders of Presbytery as guests of Dardenne.

Mr. Bunce was out of the pulpit July 13, 20 August 24, 31. The Sunday July 13 was conducted by the Presbyteens, Rev. Timothy I. Croft, who was ordained during the recent meeting of Presbytery at Dardenne church, was the preacher July 20. Rev. Timothy Croft a member of Central Presbyterian church, and a graduate of Louisville Presbyterian Seminary. He will leave shortly with his wife for Scotland where he will study at the University of Edinburgh under a fellowship in doctrinal theology, which was awarded by the seminary for superior work in his studies, August 24, the women of the church conducted the service. August 31, Mr. Donald Pomeroy was the preacher, Donald preaches regularly in the North Lincoln Westminster Parish of the United Presbyterian Church.

Annual ice-cream social July 26, 1969 at 7 p.m.

The Presbytery of St. Louis holds its fall meeting at 3 p.m. Tuesday, September 23 at Bonhomme Presbyterian Church in Chesterfield, Missouri. The recent action of our congregation, in approving the action of our session requesting Presbytery to proceed with all possible haste to the re-ordination of Mr. Bunce to the ministry is expected to be considered at this meeting.

Our Annual Homecoming September 21, 1969, Sunday School; Morning Worship; Fellowship dinner on the lawn; Special service at 1:30 p.m. Rev. Sam Rochester of Midland Presbyterian Church was our speaker.

October 5, 1969 Communion Service with Rev. Donald Archibald administering the Sacrament.

November 9, 1969 guest Minister, Rev. Donald Archibald, assistant minister of Central Presbyterian church was in the pulpit in the absence of Mr. Charles Bunce, who with his family are in Paducah, Kentucky where he is speaking twice where he served as pastor from 1945-1958. Another guest is Cindy Green a member of Central Presbyterian Church, who is our organist in the absence of Miss Sally Watson and Miss Janice Mouser. Cindy was our organist during the summer.

Our celebration of Christ's Birthday in the church December 21 Morning Worship Service. The choir sang six anthems including some favorites sung the previous year and the year before that. The Christmas family service December 24, 1969.

January 25, 1970: Ruling Elders Class 1973: Mr. Harold Keesling, Mr. Clyde Mouser, Mr. John B. Wilson. Deacons Class 1973: Gerald Aubuchon, Joseph Nielson, Mr. Edward Widowski. Deacon Class 1971 to fill unexpired term of Mr. Fred Walter, James C. Mouser. Other Ruling Elders who continue to serve on the Session are Mr. Charles Bunce, Mr. Owen England, Mrs. Jane Elzea, Mr. Philip Salvati, Mr. Vern Stewart, Miss Sally Watson. Other Deacons who continue to serve on the Board of Deacons are Mr. Cecil Barber, Mr. Ralph Cherry, Mr. Louis Comfort, Mr. Edward Kimmel, and Mr. William Kinner. In addition to those church officers who are subject to term service, Mr. Melvin Bowman and Mr. Curtis Snyder who are Elders for Life. Mrs. Willie Harris is a Deacon for Life.

Sunday, February 22, 1970 at 5 p.m. a family night supper and program was held at Weldon Springs United Church of Christ, on Highway 94 near US 40-61. Following the dinner, the youth of the host church along with a member of Dardenne, who had the lead part, presented a program "Take Time For Christ".

March 1, 1970 All church officers and church school teachers and officers attended the church officer training seminar. Leaders for the Seminar included Rev. Donald Archibald, our moderator and assistant pastor at Central Presbyterian Church; Rev. Vern Trueblood, our pastor at Kirk of the Hills Presbyterian Church; Rev. Sam Rochester, pastor of Midland Presbyterian Church. Two of the topics to be discussed include "The Spiritual Life of Church officers and leaders" and "Church officers and leaders in Evangelism". In addition there was separate discussion groups for Elders, Deacons and teachers. Supper. Another leader was Mr. B.J. Brugge.

The meaning of Lent for Presbyterians; until about thirty years ago, Lent for Presbyterians was a time when they watched their Roman Catholic, Episcopal and Lutheran friends go to church more often, and practice fasting and self denial as the fulfilling of a religious obligation.

Then in the early 1940's along with many other Protestants with less-liturgical tradition, Presbyterians began to see that this seven week season preceding Easter offers an excellant [sic] for all Christians to grow in their faith a and find new ways to express it in their daily lives.

This is the meaning of Lent for Presbyterians-not an obligation but an opportunity. Its observance is not compulsory, but voluntary. Its emphasis is not negative, but quite positive. It can be well used by all of us for such things as

(a) Re-examining our historic Christian faith

(b) Examining our personal lives in relation to our faith

(c) Rededicating ourselves to a dynamic expression of our faith in our daily lives.

(d) Making some significant sacrifice for a worthy cause.

Our Lenten Schedule of services: Sunday Morning worship theme "Great Affirmations of the Christian Faith", Maundy Thursday, March 26, Communion and reception of new members.

A new baptismal font was given the church by the Harold Keesling family, in memory of their son Gerald Keesling, who was killed in action in Vietnam in November 1969. The font was dedicated during the Maundy Thursday service. It was used for the first time in the baptism of Gerald's sister, Lina Marie Keesling along with Mark Alexander and Jeanne Rockenstein. Several other matching pieces for the church chancel will be given by the Keesling Family.

May 17, 1970, Pentecost Sunday Communion with Rev. Donald Archibald of Central Church. His wife, Norma Jean Archibald sang a solo.

May 21, Presbytery of Southeast Missouri meeting at Cape Girardeau, Missouri, unanimously received Mr. Bunce under its care as a candidate for the Gospel Ministry. This was the first step toward his re-ordination in the Presbyterian church. U.S. (He was a minister in the United Presbyterian church for 20 years and voluntarily left the ministry several years ago.) The Presbytery's action was to excuse him from the requirements for knowledge of the Greek and Hebrew language, and to assign him a thesis and an exegesis in English.

May 31, 1970 Rev. Donald Archibald of Central Church, in the absence of Mr. Bunce, who with his family are in Denver where he will report the sessions of the Southern Baptist convention for the Post-Dispatch paper, St. Louis, Missouri.

June 8-12 Vacation Church School with Mrs. Gwyneth Kinner as leader and Mrs. June Bunce as co-leader. Closing exercises were on Sunday June 14, at Morning Worship.

Rev. Dr. Lloyd B. Harmon, former pastor of Florissant Presbyterian church and teacher of the Bible at Lindenwood College, St. Charles, Missouri, preached the sermon on June 21, 1970. He is now retired and living in St. Charles, Missouri.

Youth Sunday, June 28, 1970, Presbyteens in charge, "The Gospel in a Changing World".

Groundbreaking for our new educational building was held July 5, 1970. The service was conducted by Rev. Donald Archibald and Mr. Charles Bunce. Everyone present turned a shovel of dirt. (Watson Hall)

Annual ice-cream social was held August 2, 1970.

Communion was held August 23 with Rev. Donald M. Megahan, associate pastor at Central Presbyterian Church Clayton, Missouri was with us to bring the meditation and administer the Sacrament.

September 29, 1970, Congregational meeting to call Mr. Charles M. Bunce to be Dardenne's full time pastor. Unanimous action of the congregation with 83

members present and voting 151st Anniversary Service sermon by Rev. Andrew A. Jumper, Senior pastor of Central Presbyterian Church speaker for the afternoon service "Power For The Twentieth Century": Morning Service, Rev. Donald Archibald, sermon "The Symphony of God." Congregational meeting following service. Family dinner out on the lawn.

October 4, 1970 Officers and teachers of the Sunday School were installed at 9:30 a.m. At this time the whole Sunday School went to Gospel Light Material. Morning Worship Service was Preparatory for the afternoon communion service.

A Commission of Presbytery of Southeast Missouri ordained Mr. Charles M. Bunce, October 4, 1970. Members of the commission were Rev. Sam Rochester, chairman, presiding officer, is pastor of Midland Presbyterian church; Rev. James Duncan is pastor of Troy Presbyterian church, Troy, Missouri and former moderator of Dardenne; Rev. Donald Megahan is associate pastor of Central Presbyterian church, Clayton, Missouri., Rev. Donald Archibald is assistant pastor of Central Presbyterian church and moderator of Dardenne Presbyterian church until now. The Rev. Dr. Herbert H. Watson, now retired, former supply minister of Dardenne, and a boyhood member of Dardenne. All these men have been long-time friends of Dardenne and strong supporters of its program. Ruling Elders, members of the commission were Mr. Victor Klarich, Kirk of the Hills; Mr. Lloyd Wion Overland Presbyterian church, Overland, Missouri; Mr. Thomas Croft Central Presbyterian church, Clayton, Missouri; Mr. Curtis Snyder Elder for Life, Dardenne Presbyterian church. Mrs. Kathleen Fowler King, minister of music at Central church was the organist. In the afternoon service after Mr. Bunce was ordained, he administered Holy Communion. A reception and Buffet dinner, honoring our pastor and his family and members of the commission was held at Immaculate Conception Catholic Church, Dardenne, Missouri. The reception and dinner was prepared by the women of Dardenne Presbyterian Church. In the morning service, Rev. Donald Archibald sang a Solo "How Beautiful Upon The Mountains".

By unanimous vote of the session, our new education building was named Watson Hall. In memory of the Rev. Thomas Watson and the Rev. Samuel McCluer Watson, the father and son who were pastors of Dardenne Church for more than 80 years, and also in honor of Dr. Herbert H. Watson who helped to reactivate the church in 1966.

A Union Service for outlying churches ain [sic] St. Charles County was held at Dardenne on Wednesday November 25, at 7:30 p.m. The Emmanuel United Church of Christ, Weldon Springs, Missouri and the two United churches of Christ at New Melle, Missouri took part in this service. Combined choirs took part in the service. Rev. Stephen Hussing, pastor of Emmanuel Church gave the sermon; Rev. Charles M. Bunce conducted the service; Rev. Carl Priepke gave the scripture reading and the Litany and Benediction; Mrs. Stella Hussing, organist; Mr. Philip Salvati choir director.

The dedication of Watson Hall was on December 13, 1970, Rev. Dr. Lawrence I. Stell, executive secretary of the general council of the Presbyterian church U.S. was the guest speaker at the morning service and at the dedication service in the afternoon. Fellowship dinner at 12:30 p.m. Others taking part in the dedication: Rev. Lindy M. Cannon, moderator of Presbytery; Rev. Donald Archibald and Rev. Charles M. Bunce also participated in the service. Also on the program Rev. Dr. Herbert H. Watson and Mr. Clyde Mouser, Mr. John B. Wilson.

Morning Service December 20, 1970 the choir gave their Cantata "God In a Star". Church school program "Unto Us Is Born This Day A Savior" 6:30 p.m. A Christmas Eve Communion Service was on Thursday, December 24 at 7:00 p.m. A Candlelight Watchnight Service was held December 31 at 11:00 p.m. There was a social hour for the Junior and Senior Presbyteens and the Adults before the service.

The Presbyteens-1970

Many of our current church leaders began as Presbyteens. The Dardenne group was begun when Rev. Charles Bunce was pastor, and was the forerunner of what we now know as the group of energetic young adults re-named The Tide. As individuals dedicated to the Lord and collectively, they are seen filling the front pews on Sunday morning, taking up duties with the Minutemen, working in such diverse ministries as The Community Hope Center, City Lights and on mission trips to Mexico, Haiti and recently, Bagdad, Kentucky.

DARDENNE PRESBYTERIAN CHURCH
PRESBYTEENS
1970

The youth of the Church formed a young peoples group, which they named Presbyteens. It was formed on June 25, 1967. Junior High and Senior High were included. The planning committee was in charge of the meetings till September when officers were chosen. The planning committee consisted of Sue Tipps, Tim Dutton, Dennis Stewart and Verna Gene Stone. In September officers chosen were:

President—Linda Comfort; Vice President—Sue Tipps; Secretary—Verna Gene Stone; Treasurer—Tim Dutton.

Program Committee—Carol Wilson, chairman: Janice Mouser, Lawrence England, Timothy Dutton, Elaine Cherry.

Fellowship Committee—Jean Mouser, chairman; David Miller, Cynthia Lindner, Joyce England, Michele Salvati.

Service Committee—Dennis Stewart, chairman; Shirley Comfort, Colleen Dutton, Sue Tipps, Dawn Cherry.

One of the first things this group did was to submit designs to the Session for the signs that were to be put up in front of the church and at other corners of the area. Lawrence England's design was chosen. Then came the painting and putting the signs around.

The group visited many churches. The first was the United Hebrew Temple on December 3, 1967.

December 17, 1967 they packed a box to be sent to Vietnam. Then went caroling to the shut-ins in our church.

Mr. and Mrs. Donald Pomeroy became the Advisors to the Presbyteens.

January 21, 1968 The Presbyteens toured several Roman Catholic Churches in St. Louis. The old Cathedral at the riverfront was one of them.

January 28, 1968 the Presbyteens attended an Interfaith Hootnanny at the Hope Presbyterian Church in Creve Couer, Missouri.

February 11, 1968 the Presbyteens went to Immaculate Conception Catholic Church, Dardenne, Missouri where Pastor Rev. Walter J. Fuchs discussed the Roman Catholic Faith.

February 25, 1968 The Presbyteens went to Immaculate conception Church for dinner and a joint meeting.

August 25, 1968 the Presbyteens had complete charge of the morning service. Youth Sunday, these members took part. Dennis Stewart-Call to Worship and the Invocation. Elaine Cherry read the

Old Testament and Assurance of Pardon. Carol Wilson read the New Testament reading, Romans 1:8-15 and the Apostles Creed. Lawrence England had the Morning Prayers and the Lords Prayer. David Miller had the Children's Story for the Junior Church. Gayle Cherry took care of the announcements, attendance registration, and presentation of our Tithes and Offerings. Joyce England had the Doxology and prayer of Dedication. The messages were brought by Jean Mouser, Topic-"Youth and the Church in Education." Michele Salvati-"Youth and the Church in Daily Life. Linda Comfort-"Youth and the Church in Worship" Closing Prayer and Ascription-Karen Pomeroy. The Benediction-Dennis Stewart. Greeters were-Elizabeth Kramer, Verna Gene Stone. Ushers were—Dawn Cherry, Verna Gene Stone.

In September 1968 new Officers were chosen: President-Michele Salvati.—-Vice President—David Miller—-Secretary—Jean Mouser.—-Treasurer-Joyce England.

During this time it was decided to divide the group, Junior Presbyteens and Senior Presbyteens. Outside of a few social hours no trips were made.

In September 1969 new Officers were chosen: President-Dennis Stewart—-Vice-President-Joyce England—-Secretary-Janice Mouser—-Treasurer-Lawrence England.

Fellowship Committee-Peggy Nielson, chairman-Elizabeth Kramer, Verna Gene Stone, James Stokes, Jr.

Program Committee-Joyce England, chairman-Nancy Nielson, Lawrence England.

Service Committee-Sue Tipps, chairman—Linda Comfort, Janice Mouser, Dawn Cherry.

Advisors-Mr. and Mrs. James Stokes, Sr.

Junior Presbyteens: President: Twana Alexander—-Vice President-Thomas Stone—Secretary-Nancy Stokes—-Treasurer-Audrey Kramer.

Advisors: Mr. and Mrs. Owen England.

Annual Youth Sunday Service was on September 14, 1969.

Organist: Janice Mouser

Pianist: Audrey Kramer

Greeters: Elizabeth Kramer, Thomas Stone

Ushers: Sue Tipps, James Stokes, Jr.

Call to Worship: Dawn Cherry

Call to Confession: Nancy Nielson

Scripture reading: Richard Stewart—Psalm 8:1-9 and the Apostles Creed.

Morning Prayers and the Lords Prayer-Joyce England

Children's Story: Twana Alexander

Announcements and Attendance and registration-Nancy Stokes

Presentation of Tithes and Offerings-Jean Mouser, also Doxology and Prayer of Dedication.

The main topic was "Christian Faith in the Space Age."

"Is the Christian Faith Adequate for the Space Age."-Dennis Stewart

"Is Space Exploration Contrary to God's Will?"-Verna Gene Stone

"How Can the Church Equip Us for Living in the Space Age?"-David Miller

"How Will the Space Age Change the Church?"—Lawrence England.

Installation of Presbyteen Officers and Recognition of Youth Advisors.

Presbyteens went to Whispering Hills Bible Camp, St. James, Missouri Along with six other churches, November 14-16, 1969. Twelve or our Presbyteens went to the camp.

Officers for Senior Presbyteens for 1970 were:

President-Teresa Cain

Vice President-Joyce England

Secretary-Verna Gene Stone

Treasurer-Timothy Schacher.

Officers for Junior Presbyteens for 1970 were:

President-Richard Cain

Vice-President-Scott Wright

Secretary-Faith Ann Rockenstein

Treasurer-Peggy Widowski.

March 8, 1970, Parent-Teenager Relationships, subject of panel discussion, sponsored by Senior High. All parents and Teenagers invited.

Junior High group, April 5, went to Fort Zumwalt State Park for wiener roast.

Senior High group met at the home of Mr. Charles Bunce for a spaghetti dinner, April 12, 1970.

Junior and Senior High Presbyteens met at the church May 3, their speaker was Damion Obika, a native of the former state of Biafra in Nigeria. Who will speak on the "Current Nigerian-Biafran situation." A graduate of the University of Missouri School of Journalism. Mr. Obika was a Staff reporter at the Post Dispatch, St. Louis, Missouri.

June 28 Youth Sunday-messages:

"The Gospel in a Changing World".

"How the World is Changing"-Cheri Stone

"Must the Gospel Be Changed To Meet The World's Needs?"-Teresa Cain

"The Gospel is Adequate For the Needs of the World."—Dennis Stewart

August 1, 1970 the Junior and Senior Presbyteens took an offering for the benefit of a Nigerian College Student.

Junior and Senior Presbyteens met at the Rockenstein home for a Vesper Service and wiener roast.

Fall retreat for Junior and Senior Highs held in conjunction with Kirk of the Hills, Central, Midland, Kingsland and other churches at Arcadia Bible Camp. 22 teenagers from Dardenne went.

November 22, 1970 Junior and Senior High program "Preacher On The Spot". Senior High Presbyteens made plaques which they took to the Nursing Home. Molly Wells, and they also sang carols for them, December 20th.

Social for both Junior and Senior Presbyteens in Watson Hall before the Watchnight Candlelight Service, December 31, 1970.

Chapter 11

The Dardenne Cemeteries

In June 2004, Mr. Jim Mouser—Facilities Manager for Dardenne—produced the following information on the cemeteries. While the listing of the old Dardenne Creek location is easily read, the Rock Church plot is not as clear. The list of names for the Rock Church Cemetery has been set to match the type of this book.

Tradition holds that a portion of the Rock Church site was set aside for travelers going west. The majority of pioneer travel to the west occurred prior to the Civil War, and the Rock Church was not built until several years after the War. While the plot map makes no mention of travelers, it does indicate a space for "Strangers." There are no headstones, no records, save for a few names on the plot map.

The only "Strangers" listed are: William Setson, Elroy Lawson, Ralph Lawson, Vilonia Halcomb, and *[illegible]*.

Since 1868 the Rock Church Cemetery has been the final resting place for many beloved Dardenne members.

Creek Cemetery (Bush Wildlife)

cem	num	lastname	firstname	middle	title	dob	dod	age	comments
ddn cr	1	Alexander	James	H.		07 Sep 1789	04 Sep 1835	45 y 11 m 28 d	45y 11m 27d
ddn cr	2	Alexander	Nancy	M.		17 Jul 1794	27 Aug 1833	39 y 1 m 10 d	born Rockbridge Co VA
ddn cr	3	Archer	Alexander	Shore		04 Apr 1840	20 Feb 1851	10 y 16 m 16 d	son of Edward E. and Mary Ann
ddn cr	4	Audraine	Nannie	Constance		31 Dec 1840	29-Mar-13	73 y 1 m 29 d	
ddn cr	5	Bailey	Ellens	A.		22 Jul 1853	22 Jul 1897	44 y 0 m 0 d	d. at Quogue N.Y. 44yr
ddn cr	6	Bailey	Ellsworth			30 May 1861	30 Apr 1862	0 y 11 m 0 d	infant son of Bob T. and Ann P. 11m
ddn cr	7	Bailey	Lucinda	Zumwalt		04 Nov 1812	04 Nov 1896	84 y 0 m 0 d	D. St. Charles MO 84y
ddn cr	8	Bailey	Robert	Sr.		30 Apr 1814	07 Dec 1868	54 y 7 m 8 d	54y 7m 7d
ddn cr	9	Bailey	Robert	Jr.	Cap		17 May 1864	27 y x m x d	d. Port Hudson LA in US Service / 27th yr
ddn cr	10	Belle	Thomas	G.		13 Jan 1790	13 Jan 1853	63 y 0 m 0 d	63y
ddn cr	11	Baugh	Mary Anne				22 Dec 1863	1863 y 9 m 22 d	wife of H.S.
ddn cr	12	Bigelow	George	H.		08 Jan 1853	8-Jan-35	82 y 0 m 0 d	w/Sarah
ddn cr	13	Bigelow	Sarah	A.		13 Oct 1866	28-Aug-58	92 y 10 m 15 d	h/George
ddn cr	14	Bishop	Zebada	E.		05 May 1827	26 Apr 1866	38 y 11 m 20 d	38y 11m 20d
ddn cr	15	Boyd	Elizabeth	D.		23 Sep 1782	23 Sep 1855	73 y 0 m 0 d	in 73rd year of her age
ddn cr	16	Boyd	James	R.		08 May 1838	07 Jul 1871	32 y 7 m 30 d	32y 7m 30d
ddn cr	17	Boyd	Sarah	W.		25 Dec 1845	21-Feb-32	86 y 1 m 27 d	
ddn cr	18	Brook	Edward	T.		24 Jan 1885	24 Jul 1885	0 y 6 m 0 d	son of J.W. and S.A. 6m
ddn cr	19	Callaway	Carr	D.		30 Jul 1888	04 Jan 1891	2 y 5 m 8 d	son of W.C. and H.P. 2y 5m 4d
ddn cr	20	Callaway	Cora	M.		18 Jul 1872	14 Sep 1886	14 y 1 m 27 d	dau of W.C. and H.P. 14y 1m 26d
ddn cr	21	Callaway	H.	P.		20 Jul 1845	21-Jul-17	72 y 0 m 1 d	w/W.C. his wife
ddn cr	22	Callaway	Hattie	H.		13 Nov 1871	06 Jan 1872	0 y 1 m 24 d	1m 23d
ddn cr	23	Callaway	Jimmie			27 Sep 1883	13 Jan 1901	17 y 3 m 17 d	
ddn cr	24	Callaway	Malinda			18 Mar 1819	20 Dec 1881	62 y 9 m 2 d	wife of Wm. B
ddn cr	25	Callaway	Martha	Z.		30 Nov 1881	30-Nov-56	75 y 0 m 0 d	
ddn cr	26	Callaway	W.	C.		22 Feb 1844	7-Feb-17	72 y 11 m 16 d	w/ H. P.
ddn cr	27	Callaway	William	Boone		20 Apr 1807	13 Aug 1889	82 y 3 m 24 d	
ddn cr	28	Campbell	Alex	R.	B	03 Aug 1802	21 Oct 1845	43 y 2 m 18 d	63y 2m 18d

3/28/03

Creek Cemetery (Bush Wildlife)

ddn cr	29	Campbell	Sarah	A.		01 Apr 1818	07 Nov 1899	81 y 7 m 6 d	81y 7m 6d
ddn cr	30	Campbell	William	M.		18 Jun 1775	31 Dec 1819	44 y 6 m 13 d	44y 6m 13d
ddn cr	31	Castello	Willie	Lee		19 Nov 1863	21 Sep 1885	21 y 10 m 2 d	dau of H.B. and Eliza A 21y 10m 2d
ddn cr	32	Castely	Albert	J.		08 Feb 1850	09 Dec 1855	5 y 10 m 4 d	son of John and Mary 5y 10m 2d
ddn cr	33	Castlio	Edward	C.		22 Feb 1847	29 Apr 1908	51 y 2 m 7 d	
ddn cr	34	Castlio	Eliza	Ann		21 May 1834	17 Feb 1866	31 y 8 m 27 d	wife of H.B. 31y 8m 26
ddn cr	35	Castlio	Emmet	McD.		03 Jan 1866	15 May 1895	29 y 4 m 12 d	
ddn cr	36	Castlio	Hiram	B.		09 Mar 1826	15-Nov-04	78 y 8 m 6 d	
ddn cr	37	Castlio	J.	O.		20 Nov 1859	08 Mar 1893	33 y 3 m 19 d	
ddn cr	38	Castlio	John	O		12 Jun 1819	01 Mar 1894	74 y 8 m 20 d	
ddn cr	39	Castlio	Mary	E.		03 Jul 1821	28 Feb 1896	74 y 7 m 25 d	wife of J.O.
ddn cr	40	Castlio	Mary	Rebecca		30 Nov 1859	30-Mar-33	74 y 0 m 0 d	w/William M "sister"
ddn cr	41	Castlio	Milton			24 Jan 1887	27 Sep 1887	0 y 8 m 3 d	son of J.O. and M.E.
ddn cr	42	Castlio	William	M.		30 Nov 1850	30-Nov-20	70 y 0 m 0 d	brother w/Mary k
ddn cr	43	Castlio	Zerelda	E. D.		16 Jul 1803	28 Dec 1803	0 y 5 m 16 d	dau of J.O. and M.E.
ddn cr	44	Clare	Saturn			17 Dec 1849	17 Dec 1862	13 y 0 m 0 d	dau of N and B 13y 313d
ddn cr	45	Conaulay	David	B.		25 Dec 1817	19 Aug 1835	37 y 7 m 25 d	son of A. and W
ddn cr	46	Cunningham	James	H.		22 May 1832	12 Nov 1844	12 y 5 m 21 d	12y 8m 13c
ddn cr	47	Gamble	Achillia	A.		01 Feb 1852	21-Sep-04	52 y 7 m 20 d	beloved wife of R.E. 52y 7m 20d
ddn cr	48	Gamble	Rufus	E.		19 Jan 1840	1-Mar-09	69 y 4 m 13 d	w/Achillia 69y 1m 11d
ddn cr	49	Gill	John			27 Feb 1780	28 Jan 1872	91 y 11 m 1 d	
ddn cr	50	Gill	Peter	W.		02 Sep 1816	05 Dec 1846	30 y 3 m 3 d	30y 3m 3d
ddn cr	51	Hays	Daniel	B.		21 Mar 1866	23-Mar-10	42 y 3 m 2 d	wife:Serena
ddn cr	52	Hays	Lois	C.		24 May 1891	5-Feb-06	14 y 8 m 13 d	
ddn cr	53	Hays	Serena	C.		11 May 1860	5-Apr-36	75 y 10 m 25 d	wife of Daniel
ddn cr	54	Hedrick	Nancy	B.		19 Nov 1818	19 Nov 1871	53 y 0 m 0 d	53y
ddn cr	55	Hedrick	Polley	F.		04 Jul 1848	26 Mar 1870	21 y 8 m 22 d	
ddn cr	56	Hensall	David			30 Nov 1791	30 Nov 1843	52 y 0 m 0 d	52y
ddn cr	57	Hensall	David	L.		23 Feb 1829	23 Feb 1840	11 y 0 m 0 d	11y

2

3/28/03

Creek Cemetery (Bush Wildlife)

ddn cr	58	Henwell	Nancy	C.	18 Oct 1791	09 Mar 1865	73 y 4 m 22 d	73y 4m 21d
ddn cr	80	Hillar	Jacob		28 Jul 1818	20 Oct 1867	49 y 2 m 23 d	49y 2m 22d
ddn cr	59	Howell	Almarinda		25 Dec 1840	13 Oct 1860	19 y 9 m 19 d	dau of J and S 19y 9m 18d
ddn cr	62	Howell	John	B.	28 Feb 1856	03 Nov 1869	13 y 8 m 6 d	son of Tho A. & Sara J 13y 8m 8d
ddn cr	61	Howell	Joanna		10 Dec 1789	01 Jan 1861	71 y 0 m 22 d	wife of John 71y 21d
ddn cr	62	Howell	John		09 Sep 1781	25 Feb 1869	87 y 5 m 16 d	
ddn cr	64	Howell	Lewis		22 May 1800	18 Dec 1876	76 y 6 m 27 d	76y 6m 26d
ddn cr	63	Howell	Isadora	V	30 Jul 1853	11 Oct 1869	16 y 2 m 12 d	dau of Tho.A & Sarah 16y 2m 11d
ddn cr	65	Howell	Sarah	Rosalin	14 Oct 1849	12-May-11		dau of Lewis and Serena L.
ddn cr	66	Howell	Serena	L.	22 May 1806	05 Apr 1882	75 y 10 m 14 d	wife of Lewis 75y 10m 13d
ddn cr	67	Hutchings	Infant		24 May 1863	30 May 1863	0 y 0 m 8 d	dau of C & J 8 days
ddn cr	68	Hutchings	Jane		05 Aug 1839	01 Jun 1863	23 y 9 m 27 d	wife of C. Jr. 23y 9m 26d
ddn cr	69	Irman	Laura	Alice	15 Dec 1854	16 Feb 1891	36 y 2 m 1 d	
ddn cr	121	Ireward	Isaac		02 Apr 1873	10-Mar-33	59 y 11 m 8 d	wife was Mabel
ddn cr	70	King	Perth	A	13 Feb 1854	09 Sep 1854	0 y 6 m 27 d	dau of Robert & Mary
ddn cr	71	Long	John	H	12 Jul 1864	12-Jul-25	61 y 0 m 0 d	50Y
ddn cr	72	Long	Mattie		01 Jun 1866	1-Apr-30	63 y 10 m 0 d	63y 10m
ddn cr	73	Matthews	George	W.	24 Nov 1833	02 Mar 1844	10 y 3 m 9 d	son of E.P. & M.B. 10y 3m 8d
ddn cr	74	Mockuer	John	M.	08 Feb 1822	29 Sep 1834	12 y 7 m 21 d	12y 7m 21d
ddn cr	75	Mockuer	Robert		11 Apr 1792	21 Sep 1834	42 y 5 m 10 d	42y 5m 10d
ddn cr	76	Mockuer	Robert		29 Apr 1792	21 Sep 1834	42 y 4 m 23 d	WifeSophia
ddn cr	77	Mockuer	Sally	C.	06 May 1820	30 Aug 1833	13 y 3 m 24 d	dau of Robert and Sophis
ddn cr	78	Mockuer	Sophia	C.	22 Jun 1795	02 Jan 1867	71 y 6 m 11 d	wife of R same stone
ddn cr	79	Miller	Elizabeth		13 Jul 1820	18 Apr 1900	79 y 9 m 5 d	wife of Jacob 79y 9m 5d
ddn cr	81	Moore	Ann Pines		09 Jun 1841	4-Aug-26	85 y 1 m 26 d	
ddn cr	82	Moore	Cathadine		31 Jan 1807	01 Aug 1892	85 y 6 m 1 d	WIFE of J.D. (same stone)
ddn cr	83	Moore	Emily	W.	02 Jun 1847	22 Jun 1860	13 y 0 m 20 d	dau of J.L. & M. 13y 20d
ddn cr	84	Moore	James	D.	15 Mar 1802	19 May 1896	94 y 2 m 4 d	W/Catharine
ddn cr	85	Moore	James	D. Jr.	07 Dec 1839	20-May-05	65 y 5 m 13 d	

3

Creek Cemetery (Bush Wildlife)

ddn cr	86	Moore	John	L.	10 Dec 1811	17 Jan 1867	55 y 1 m 7 d	55y 1m 7d
ddn cr	87	Moore	Joseph	W.	14 Oct 1826	16 Apr 04	77 y 6 m 2 d	77y 6m 2d
ddn cr	88	Moore	Melinda		16 Mar 1823	31 Jan 1901	77 y 10 m 15 d	wife of John L.
ddn cr	89	Mound	Andrew		12 Apr 1828	12 Apr 1860	32 y 0 m 0 d	in his 32nd year
ddn cr	90	Muschany	Cetilus	J.	10 Nov 1841	08 Jan 1842	0 y 1 m 29 d	
ddn cr	91	Muschany	Charlie	Legrand	16 Sep 1853	16 Mar 1856	2 y 6 m 0 d	son of J.B. & J.
ddn cr	92	Muschany	Children					S.C. & Virginia no dates
ddn cr	94	Muschany	John	B.	07 Jun 1806	02 Jan 1862	55 y 6 m 26 d	w/Janetta 55y 6m 25d
ddn cr	95	Muschany	Virginia		30 Sep 1842	29 Jan 1871	28 y 3 m 30 d	wife of S. G. 28y 3m 30d
ddn cr	93	Muschany	Izedila	C.	02 Oct 1817	11 Jan 1880	62 y 3 m 9 d	wife of John B. 62y 3m 9d
ddn cr	96	Neison	John		02 Dec 1860	02 Dec 1863	3 y 0 m 0 d	3 years
ddn cr	97	Pitman	Infant					child of J.B and B.
ddn cr	98	Salone	Salone		16 Apr 1831	30 Apr 1865	34 y 0 m 15 d	wife of JOHN B.
ddn cr	99	Pace	Absalom	C.	22 Aug 1817	15 Jul 1878	60 y 10 m 24 d	
ddn cr	100	Price	Margaret	J.	29 Aug 1821	08 Aug 1877	55 y 11 m 9 d	wife of A. C.
ddn cr	101	Quald	Anne	M.	13 Feb 1852	16 Dec 1852	0 y 10 m 3 d	daughter of WM and Ann
ddn cr	102	Quald	Mary	H.	13 Feb 1857	16 Dec 1857	0 y 10 m 3 d	daughter of WM and Ann
ddn cr	103	Scherbauer	Ellen	Stevenson	09 Apr 1860	17 Apr 1886	26 y 0 m 8 d	
ddn cr	104	Stevenson	Alice		23 May 1975	5-Jun-66	91 y 0 m 13 d	
ddn cr	105	Stevenson	George		11 Nov 1856	18 Apr 1867	10 y 5 m 7 d	
ddn cr	106	Stevenson	George		07 May 1802	07 Jan 1864	61 y 7 m 11 d	61y 7m 10d
ddn cr	107	Stevenson	Mathilda	L.	21 Oct 1874	5-Feb-09	34 y 3 m 15 d	w/ William R.
ddn cr	108	Stevenson	Sarah		16 Jan 1831	16 Feb 1901	70 y 1 m 0 d	husband George 70y 1m
ddn cr	109	Stevenson	William	R.	25 Aug 1862	29-Oct-12	45 y 2 m 4 d	wife Mathilda
ddn cr	110	Stewart	Addale		08 Oct 1867	3-Jul-31	63 y 8 m 25 d	wife Cecil
ddn cr	111	Stewart	Alice	Madore	23 Jul 1852	23 Sep 1853	1 y 0 m 0 d	daughter of E.C. and A. 1y 2m
ddn cr	112	Stewart	Arthurs	A.		15 Aug 1846	1846 y 6 m 15 d	daughter of E.C. and L.
ddn cr	113	Stewart	Cecil	C.	14 Feb 1861	5-Aug-43	82 y 5 m 22 d	wife Addale
ddn cr	114	Stewart	Cosnza	U.	30 Nov 1846	30-Nov-21	81 y 0 m 0 d	

4

Creek Cemetery (Bush Wildlife)

ddn cr	115	Stewart	Darthula	A.	30 Oct 1847	17 May 1854	6 y 6 m 18 d	daughter of E.C. and L. 6y 6m 17d
ddn cr	116	Stewart	Francis	H	18 Mar 1810	23 Jul 1888	78 y 4 m 5 d	wife Louise A. 78y 4m 5d
ddn cr	117	Stewart	Francis	P.	30 Nov 1869	30-Nov-49	80 y 0 m 0 d	check dates
ddn cr	118	Stewart	George	C	11 Nov 1850	07 Mar 1852	1 y 3 m 27 d	son of E.C. and L. 1y 3m 26d
ddn cr	120	Stewart	Isaac	Calvert	01 Apr 1854	13 Mar 1855	0 y 11 m 12 d	son of E.C. and L. 11m 12d
ddn cr	122	Stewart	James	F	30 Nov 1836	30-Nov-14	78 y 0 m 0 d	wife was Coaxus B.
ddn cr	119	Stewart	Infant Babe		23 Oct 1887	01 Nov 1887	0 y 0 m 9 d	daughter of C.C. and J.A. 8 days
ddn cr	123	Stewart	Louess	Bell	30 Jan 1857	21 Mar 1861	4 y 1 m 21 d	daughter of E.C. and L.
ddn cr	124	Stewart	Louise	A.	19 Nov 1812	03 Jan 1895	82 y 1 m 15 d	wife of F.H (same stone) 82y 1m 14d
ddn cr	125	Stewart	Mabel	E.	30 Dec 1880	30-Jun-30	49 y 6 m 0 d	wife of Isaac H.
ddn cr	126	Thomas	James	W	07 Jan 1828	07 Mar 1846	18 y 2 m 0 d	son of E.B. and M.A. 18y 2m
ddn cr	127	Thompson	Blair	H	24 Jan 1824	24 Jan 1856	32 y 0 m 0 d	32y
ddn cr	128	Thompson	Blair	Y.	10 Sep 1853	31 Aug 1854	0 y 11 m 21 d	son of B.H. and H.A. 11m 21d
ddn cr	129	Thompson	Hester	A.	11 Nov 1854	06 Dec 1865	11 y 0 m 26 d	11y 25d
ddn cr	130	Trevey	June			08 Aug 1818	1818 y 6 m 8 d	wife of J.Y.
ddn cr	132	Watson	Agnes	Frayser	09 Mar 1882	18-Jan-24	41 y 10 m 9 d	
ddn cr	133	Watson	Annie	Ruffner	30 Nov 1852	30-Nov-33	81 y 0 m 0 d	wife of Rev. Samuel
ddn cr	134	Watson	Charles	Ruffner	06 Jul 1893	11-Oct-56	63 y 3 m 5 d	by Grace we are saved through faith
ddn cr	135	Watson	Jeannette	N.	16 Jun 1884	29-Mar-72	87 y 9 m 13 d	
ddn cr	136	Watson	Julia	C.	30 Jul 1888	1-Dec-88	80 y 4 m 2 d	
ddn cr	137	Watson	Nannie	Lucretia	29 Dec 1895	21-Jan-37	41 y 0 m 23 d	
ddn cr	138	Watson	Samuel	McCluer (Re	30 Nov 1850	30-Nov-24	74 y 0 m 0 d	49 years a Presbyterian minister w/Annie
ddn cr	131	Yeater	James	E.	12 Nov 1840	15 Aug 1863	22 y 9 m 3 d	22y 9m 3d

5

Dardenne Presbyterian Rock Church Cemetery Gravesites (July 2004)

Plots for which lines are shown without names, or only portions of a name, are so because those names on the gravemarkers or records are unreadable or illegible.

PLOT	OCCUPANT/OWNER	PLOT	OCCUPANT/OWNER
1	J.C. Johnson / J.M. Diehr	32	Barton Bates
2	J.A. Boyd	33	Barton Bates
3	Issac Saul	34	Barton Bates
4	Charles Diehr	35	S.C. McCluer
5	A. Fowler	36	Rev. T. Watson
6	Unmarked	37	Rev. T. Watson
7	McCluer	38	Thomas Watson
8	O. McCluer	39	Mrs. Miller
9	J.B. Gamble	40	Dr. Currier
10	A. Bradley	41	J.W. Williams
11	R.G. Woodson	42	Mr. Burch
12	W.A. Harris	43	J.A. Campbell
13	McCausland	44	T.E. Talbott
14	Lee	45	E.L. Muschany
15	Henry Watson	46	L.T. Henry
16	Mr. Doty	47	Louie McCluer
17	B.T. Gill	48	McCluer
18	W.W. Campbell	49	J.M. Wilson
19	James Hensell	50	J.H. Gilbert and Chaney
20	James Hensell	51	Herrington
21	Arthur McCluer	52	Joe and James Moore
22	R.A. McCluer	53	Will Gill
23	J.H. Hatcher	54	A. Hutchings
24	Strother Johnson	55	A.D. Holtzclaw
25	O. Holtzclaw	56	[Unknown]
26	S.L. Muschany	57	Lay and Felty
27	J.M. Wilson	58	T.B. Woods
28	J.B. Muschany	59	Tom McClenny
29	Rev. S.M. Watson	60	Stone
30	Mrs. Jennetta Muschany	61	McCluer
31	Fred Hatcher	62	McCluer

Chapter 12

A Walk Through History

The Dardenne Presbyterian Church Timeline 1560–2004

1560   The Church of Scotland is established.

1611   King James Version of the Bible is published in London.

1661   Presbyterians begin arriving in the British colonies of America.

1695   Philosopher John Locke publishes, "The Reasonableness of Christianity."

1706   Rev. Francis MacKenamie, of Londonderry, becomes the first installed minister of the first Presbyterian church at Snow Hill, Maryland.

1740   University of New Jersey, founded by Presbyterians, is later renamed Princeton University.

1762   Louis Blanchette visits the area in the Upper Louisiana Territory now known as St. Charles County.

1764   Laclede and Chouteau establish a fur trading post on Mississippi River and name it after King Louis IX of France. The town is named St. Louis.

1769   Louis Blanchette returns to the Louisiana Territory and establishes Les Petite Cotes-later known as San Carlos under Spanish rule then as St. Charles under American ownership.

1776   The American Revolution begins.

1799   Daniel Boone and a group of settlers arrive in the Femme Osage Valley of the Missouri Territory.

1800   Francis Howell arrives in the San Carlos area of the Missouri Territory. Forts Boone, Howell and Pond are built to protect settlers against Indian raids.
       Spain cedes the Louisiana Territory to France.

1803   The United States purchases the Louisiana Territory from France.

1804   President Thomas Jefferson asks William Clark and Meriwether Lewis to explore the newly acquired land.

1807   The Boone's Lick Trail is begun in order to mine the salt springs in central Missouri.
       The first Sunrise Service is held west of the Mississippi River at Belleview Settlement (later Caledonia, Missouri.)

1812   William Clark is named first governor of the Missouri Territory War begins with England.

1816   Missionary Rev. Albert Salmon Giddings arrives in St. Louis.
       Rev. Giddings establishes two churches, Belleview and Bonhomme Presbyterian Churches.

1817   Missionary Rev. Timothy Flint arrives to assist Rev. Giddings.
       The 1st Presbyterian Church at St. Louis is established.

1819   Rev. Giddings establishes churches at Shoal Creek and Edwardsville, Illinois.
       Rev. Timothy Flint requests leave of the Presbytery.
       Missionaries Rev. Charles Robinson and Rev. David Tenney arrive to assist Rev. Giddings.
       Presbytery accepts constitution prepared by Giddings, Robinson, and Tenney to form a Missionary Society in the Missouri Territory.
       Dardenne Prairie Presbyterian Church is established on September 18th.
       Rev. David Tenney dies only weeks after establishing Brazeau Presbyterian Church

1820   The Missouri Compromise.
       Daniel Boone dies.

1821   Missouri becomes the 24th State of the Union.
       Rev. Giddings establishes Apple Creek, Harkarken and Bethel Presbyterian.

1823   Rev. Giddings establishes Unionville Presbyterian Church.
       Andrew and Margaret Zumwalt gifts five acres of land near Dardenne Creek to Dardenne Presbyterian Church (Now part of Busch Wildlife area)

1827   Mrs. Mary Easton Sibley establishes a school for young women at St. Charles. (Later known as Lindenwood University.)

1830   German immigrants begin to arrive in the area.

1837   Abolitionist and Editor, Rev. Elijah P. Lovejoy is killed by Southern sympathizers.

1839   Missouri State University is established.

1840   Towns of Howell and Cottleville are settled.

1841   Femme Osage Presbyterian Church established.

1844   Rev. Thomas Watson becomes 1st installed pastor of Dardenne Presbyterian.

1845   John Nelson sells Dardenne Presbyterian two acres of land for $1.00. Includes water rights to Nelson Spring for 1,000 years.

1849   Cholera Epidemic sweeps the county.
Rev. Thomas Watson III marries Nannie McCluer, daughter of Elder, Dr. Robert McCluer.
Plank Roads are chartered in St. Charles County.

1853   Femme Osage Presbyterian Church closes. Many members join with Dardenne Presbyterian.

1856   Goebel Photography of St. Charles is established. Goebel records much of early St. Charles County history.
Pierre Foristell founds Foristell, Missouri.

1860   Abraham Lincoln elected President of the United States.

1861   Civil War begins.
Confederate sympathizers attack Union train at Wentzville.

1862   Dardenne Presbyterian Church is destroyed by fire. A brush arbor is built for services.

1865   Mechanicsville is founded by F. Castlio

1868   Judge Edward Bates gifts Dardenne Presbyterian with five acres of land located on the Boone Trail.
The Dardenne Presbyterian Rock Church is built.
Mr. Adam Lamb arrives as a tutor for the Watson children.

1870   The women of the church, organized as the Mite Society, donate a new organ to the church. Total cost: $26.

1872   Presbytery orders Dardenne congregation to divide. The sister church becomes known as "South Dardenne." The Rock Church becomes known as "Old Dardenne."
Hiram Castlio of Mechanicsville donates land for new South Dardenne church.

1880   Missouri River flood shifts the river course

1881   Howell Institute is established in Howell, Missouri. It is the forerunner of Francis Howell School District.

1888   Rev. Thomas Watson dies.

1890   Rev. Samuel M. Watson, son of Rev. Thomas Watson, becomes Stated Supply pastor to "Old Dardenne" while serving as installed pastor of "Dardenne South".
        Wooden narthex is added to the Rock Church.
1892   Rev. Samuel Watson becomes the 2nd installed pastor of Dardenne Presbyterian.
1902   O'Fallon Presbyterian Church is organized.
1904   World's Fair is held in St. Louis.
1917   America enters the First World War.
1919   Centennial Anniversary of Dardenne Presbyterian Church.
1925   Rev. Samuel Watson dies at his home in Maplewood.
1927   Charles Lindbergh flight across the Atlantic.
1929   The Stock Market crashes.
1931   Area banks begin to close in St. Charles and Warren counties.
1940   South Dardenne church closes.
1941   The United States enters World War II when Pearl Harbor is attacked.
1944   Dardenne Presbyterian celebrates 125th Anniversary.
1945   World War II ends.
1947   O'Fallon Presbyterian Church closes and donates its bell to Dardenne Presbyterian Church.
1952   Weekly worship services are discontinued at Dardenne.
1962   Dardenne Church is reopened after being closed for several years.
1964   Contract for remodeling the Rock Church is signed.
1965   Missouri Supreme Court ruling denies Dardenne Presbyterian the Castlio bequest of $10,000.
        Results of survey lead to formation of "regional concept" and new growth in Dardenne Church.
        Dardenne Presbyterian membership totals 9 members.
        Sally Watson and Allene Watson are ordained as the first women Elders in Dardenne history.
1966   Sunday School is started at Dardenne. Church membership totals 15.
        Weekly Services are re-established.
        Rev. Herbert H. Watson becomes pastor at Dardenne.
1967   Charles Bunce becomes Lay Leader of Dardenne Presbyterian.
        Clyde Mouser installed as Superintendent of Sunday School.
        Mrs. Willie Harris and Allene Watson are made Life Members of the Deacon Board. Curtis
        Snyder and Melvin Bowman are made Life Members of Elders.
        The first Vacation Bible School is held. Mrs. June Bunce is leader. There are 65 registered with 17 teachers and helpers.

Junior Church is established.

The Presbyteens are formed.

The first Ice Cream Social is held at Dardenne.

1968   Central Presbyterian offers a 2-for-1 fund raising program.

Plans are made to build an Educational Building at Dardenne (later known as Watson Hall).

The first Adult Bible Study is begun and held once a month in members' homes.

1969   Dardenne Presbyterian celebrates 150th anniversary.

Astronaut Neil Armstrong walks on the moon.

Dardenne still holds Preparatory Service for Holy Communion.

Session sets special rules should Black Militants disrupt Worship services.

Dardenne Church membership reaches 128.

1970   Rev. Charles Bunce becomes the 3rd installed pastor.

Watson Hall is completed.

1971   The Manse on Knollwood Court is purchased.

1972   The renovation of the Rock Church is completed.

1973   Rev. Charles Bunce dies.

1974   Rev. Thomas Sale becomes the 4th installed pastor at Dardenne Presbyterian Church.

1980   The 8:00 a.m. Sunday worship service is added to the schedule.

1981   Lloyd Daugherty donates $35,000 to Dardenne for a pipe organ.

1985   The Brick Church is completed.

1987   Adam Lamb Preschool is established.

1996   Rev. Gary Myers becomes the first co-pastor of Dardenne Presbyterian Church.

1997   The Lloyd Daugherty Memorial Organ is completed.

Rev. Thomas Sale retires.

1998   Rev. Gary Myers becomes the 5th installed pastor of Dardenne Presbyterian Church.

Rev. Lewis Kimmel becomes Associate Pastor at Dardenne Presbyterian Church.

2002   The Christian Life Center and Sale Library are dedicated.

The first 4-Day Mission Conference is held at Dardenne.

Marc Sikma becomes Youth Minister and "The Tide" is formed.

2004   Dardenne Presbyterian celebrates 185th anniversary.

Membership at Dardenne reaches 1,500.

The Giddings Lovejoy Presbytery membership totals 35,000 with 106 churches.

Chapter 13

Dardenne Family and Community Ministries

Adult Sunday School: Classes include different approaches to learning more about the Bible and the Christian faith. Some include a balance of Bible study and various subjects of interest. There is also one class especially for singles.

Seekers: A group of energetic people interested in a balance of Bible and thematic study.

New Dawn: This class enjoys both Bible and Christian book studies that encourage the sharing of inner spiritual lives.

Finders: A group of people ages 19-90 who are climbing the "Spiritual Hill" of life.

Pathfinders: Singles and Couples share a wealth of valuable experiences.

New Bethany: A group of people with children in their teens or older. This class has a desire for serious study of the Bible and Christian writings.

New Followers: A class for couples and singles of all ages.

New Beginnings: Singles: A class for adult singles of all ages.

Genesis: Parents of young and school-age children make up this class.

Serendipity: Format is guided discussions with the Bible as reference. Ages 25-65

Bible 101: Studying the Book of First John

The Vine: Post high school or returning college student. Singles or marrieds 19-29.

SONday School: A 19-week course on the Book of Romans. Drop in any time during course study.

Titus 2: A women's group for Bible study and discussion. Each group meets at different times and locations.

Inquiry Class: Held periodically throughout the year, this six-session class offers an opportunity to learn more about Dardenne, the Christian faith, and the Presbyterian Church. Attendees can take advantage of Sunday mornings or Wednesday evening classes.

Wednesday Evening Bible Study: Following family dinner at 6:00 p.m., Adult Bible study at 7:00 p.m. Studies of Bible, theology, church history, parenting, and marriage classes. Courses last 6-8 weeks beginning in Sept. and continue through mid-May.

Family Night: Every Wednesday night, from September to May, includes a variety of wholesome dinners for a modest price and bible classes for every member of the family.

Jesus and Men: Men of the congregation meet to study God's Word the 1st and 3rd Saturday mornings of each month and every Monday night. They also attend an annual conference and several get-togethers each year.

Presbyterian Women: Female members of the church are automatically members of PW when they join Dardenne. Circles meet monthly for Bible Study and fellowship. Additionally, they provide meals for church families during family emergencies or after funerals.

Family Life Counseling: Dardenne offers on-site counseling center for members and others.

Family Mentoring Program: Program helps families both in and outside the church to develop independent living skills.

Covenant Groups: Bible study for couples offers the opportunity for approximately six couples to a group to gather for fellowship and bible study.

St. Giles Health Program: Parish Nurse, Lisa McCluer, offers health and wellness programs. Counsels individuals on personal health care issues.

Keenagers: The "mature" members (age 50 and over) of Dardenne gather for fellowship, service and various fun projects designed for spiritual growth. They meet the third Saturday of each month for fellowship and service projects.

Annual Church Retreat: Annual retreat offers opportunity for spiritual growth and study as well as recreation at Mound Ridge Camp.

Partners in Prayer: This prayer group prays for members of the church during different times and places. A prayer calendar is distributed.

Intercessory Prayer Group: This group meets for intercessory prayer each Wednesday night throughout the year

Chancel Choir: Senior High through Adult meets on Wednesday night.

Youth Worship Team: Leads the musical portion of worship on the fifth Sunday of the month.

Dardenne Ringers: Handbell choir-Teen through Adult.

Instrumental: The Dardenne Band meets on Tuesday nights. All musicians are welcome.

Hidden Hands Puppet Ministry: A ministry for conveying Bible stories to children.

Fellowship Players: The Dardenne drama group performs several times a year. Cast, crew and stagehands are always welcome to join the group.

Nursery: Loving and dedicated attendants provide for infant and toddler care during all three worship services on Sunday and during other church events.

Adam Lamb Preschool: For preschool children of the church and community. All teachers have degrees in education. Aides have classroom experience and/or education. Continuing education is provided for all staff through classes and workshops. All staff members are CPR certified. Call the office for class times and fee structure. The goals are based on the philosophy to provide a warm, supportive atmosphere in which a child can grow academically, spiritually, socially and artistically.

Mothers Day Out: Child comes once a week on Tuesday, Wednesday, or Thursday from 9:30 a.m. to 2:30 p.m. Registration is held in March and class is available from Labor Day to Memorial Day. Call the office for details.

Sunday School classes-9:30 a.m.

Nursery: A well-staffed nursery is provided for infants and toddlers at all three worship services on Sunday mornings, Wednesday evenings and special events. Check with the church office for details.

Preschool: Children age 2 years through kindergarten are instructed in an innovative training program at their level in Christian growth using "Beginnings & Explorers" by Great Commissions Publications.

First through Sixth Grade: Our entire Sunday School uses the excellent material, "Word Action," published by Nazarene Publishing House. In addition to the solid curriculum, teachers use other resource material, videos, and crafts to enhance the children's studies. An annual Christmas program is presented by all the children involved in Sunday School.

Sunday School Hour-11:00a.m.

Nursery: Care is offered between, and during worship services on Sunday mornings and other events.

Preschool: Children age 2 through pre-kindergarten are instructed using "Word Action" materials published by the Nazarene Publishing House. Using a different curriculum at each Sunday School Hour provides variety and enrichment to children attending either Sunday School time period.

Kindergarten through Fifth Grade: Junior Church provides the opportunity for children to learn about the order, content, and purpose of the worship service. A 20-minute service includes singing, a sermon, and prayers. Recreation, crafts and refreshments follow the structured worship time.

Sunday School Outreach: Various social needs are brought to the attention of our children during the church year. Outreach programs include visiting nursing homes and donating items to needy families throughout the world.

Weekday Clubs: Bible Clubs are offered on Wednesday evenings from 7:00-8:30pm for children age 3 through the sixth grade. The fun-filled award program involves children in scripture memorization, Bible study, and Christian service projects. Bible clubs begin in September and continue through the beginning of May.

Special Events: In addition to our regular programs, various children's activities are planned throughout the church year. Movie nights, lock-ins, and parties provide children with the opportunity of fellowship with their peers at Dardenne.

Vacation Bible School: One week each summer, vacation bible school classes are designed to involve the children in exciting experiences. The Day Camps teach the beauty of God's world.

Boy Scouts of America: Cub Scouts at Dardenne learn to incorporate spiritual aspects into daily living while learning new skills.

M.A.D. Camp: Weeklong camp for Teens offers Music, Art and Drama.

Mini-M.A.D. Camp: Four-day camp offers the same program for younger members.

Choir: Five different age-appropriate levels are available:

Cherub-Ages 4 and 5

Lyric-Grades 1-3

Chi Rho-Grades 4 and 5

Salvation Singers-Grades 6 through 8

Revelation Singers-Grades 9-12

Handbell Choir: Four different handbell choirs to appeal to all age groups:

Lyric Chimes-3rd Grade

Glory Ringers-Grades 4 and 5

Praise Ringers-Grades 6 through 12

Dardenne Ringers-Teen through Adult

The TIDE-Youth Ministry: Young adults enjoy great times in activities both at the church and on trips. The Tide is an important tool for growing in the Lord during a formative time in life. Throughout the year, Dardenne offers movie nights, lock-ins and parties. Recently, mission work has included both local and foreign locales. Meets weekly on Sunday evenings and High Tide, the Bible study program gets together on Wednesday nights.

Work Camps: A weeklong volunteer opportunity each summer in a different locale. Volunteers participate in various projects to help the needy and strengthen their faith.

Annual Mission Trip: One-week trip to Tecate, Mexico to help build homes for needy families and to participate in a Vacation Bible School. Motto: To Love Is To Serve.

Local Mission Opportunities: Several mission opportunities are available at City Lights, Community Hope Center, Emmaus House and Habitat for Humanity.

Although most of the programs and mission opportunities listed below existed prior to the first Mission conference in 2002, some have evolved as a result of it. The Dardenne congregation continues to seek now opportunities to serve others and glorify God.

Alpha: An evangelizing ministry that serves a two-fold purpose. An excellent course to introduce Jesus Christ and Christianity and for those who wish to develop a deeper relationship with the Lord. Following a casual dinner, and video groups explore the life of Jesus and Christianity. Meets weekly for ten weeks. Many who come to explore stay to become leaders.

Community Hope Center: Operates a food pantry and supplies food to over 100 needy families each week. Recent expansion allows for additional help with clothing and some necessities. System allows for food and necessities to be offered in an atmosphere of generosity while allowing the recipient to retain dignity in a time of need.

St. Louis Bread Company Donations: Bread products are picked up and delivered two nights per week to Salvation Army for their Crisis Center. A minimal amount of time is required although there is some heavy lifting. A full-size car or van is desirable.

Prayer and Praise Hour: Every other Sunday the group takes worship service to nursing homes such as Twin Oaks in O'Fallon and Wentzville Park Care Center in Wentzville. Worship services are provided for senior residents. Volunteers lead prayer, singing and sharing of God's word.

Alcoholics Anonymous and ALANON: The 12-step recovery programs receive support from Dardenne. Groups meet twice a week.

Divorce Care: A nationwide outreach program. It has received an immediate and positive response from the community. The program's goal is to offer emotional and spiritual comfort with compassion and guidance during a painful and often emotionally tumultuous time.

Mary Martha Thrift Shop: Clothing and household items are collected then provided to the community as resale. Profits are distributed to needy families throughout the area.

Stephen Ministry: Trained to successfully help others with difficult personal problems this group helps in long-term situations and takes some of the workload off the ministers.

Habitat for Humanity: International and inter-denominational project that provides housing for needy families. While some construction skills are desirable they are not necessary. Volunteers are also needed to prepare and provide lunch for the workers.

The Quilters Group: Meet every Tuesday to produce beautiful quilts. Proceeds from the sales go to several mission projects.

Presbyterian Care Team: Provides practical, emotional and spiritual support to those in need. Needs may include developmental or physical disability, prolonged physical or mental illness, or life challenging situations.

Faith and Family Connections: Assists families on welfare and guides them to become self-sufficient. Requirements include a background check and a one-year commitment to the family. The goal is to see the family off welfare within one year.

Community Work Days: Periodic opportunity for all members and young adults which provides one day of work to assist area individuals and groups with various maintenance tasks.

The Minutemen: Members of congregation visit with first-time worshipers to welcome them to Dardenne and offer information about the church.

DPC Mission Conference: Annual conference presents an opportunity to learn about mission work from those in the field, to encourage support for missionaries or participation in mission trips.

New City Fellowship Work Day: Assistance is provided to New City Fellowship PCA-a multi-cultural church located in the inner city. One day a month, volunteers help with various projects which may include helping families move, rehabbing homes, or sorting clothing for the Free Store.

Bibliography

Publications

Books

Grun, Bernard, editor. *The Timetables of History.* Simon and Schuster, New York, London, Toronto, Sydney, Tokyo & Singapore. 1991. New York, NY.

Author Unknown, *Encyclopedia of the History of St. Louis*—1899. Domination French. p. 583 Domination, Spanish. p.586

378 South Western Reporter 2d Series, 1994, Supreme Court of Missouri, Estate of Earle G. Tyler Castlio. Smith v. Dardenne Presbyterian Church pp. 465-467. West Publishing Group. St. Paul, MN.

Watson, Elizabeth A. *Dardenne Presbyterian Church: Its People-Its Community.* Unpublished manuscript, 1969. St. Charles County, MO.

Watson, Elizabeth A. *Heritage and Promise: A Story of Dardenne Presbyterian Church and Its Community.* Adams Press, Chicago, IL, 1977

Periodicals

Bunce, Charles M. *News of Religion.* St. Louis Post-Dispatch, December 11, 1970. p. 16A, St. Louis, MO. (General History Archives of Dardenne Presbyterian Church, Dardenne Prairie, MO)

Corrigan, Don. *Literary and Journalistic Luminaries in St. Louis.* St. Louis Journalism Review, July/August 2002. pp. 16-19, St. Louis, MO.

Fenning, Esther Talbot. *Pioneer Days at Lindenwood.* St. Louis Post-Dispatch, St. Charles County Post. p. SC3. September 26, 2002. St. Charles, MO.

George, Alan. *Fortifications Gave First Pioneer Settlers Protection.* Wentzville Journal, October 10, 2001 p. B1. Wentzville, MO.

George, Alan. *Many Cultures Forged History of County.* Wentzville Journal, April 24, 2002. p. B1. Wentzville, MO.

Hesman, Tina. *Team Begins Excavating 1884 Steamboat Wreck.* St. Louis Post-Dispatch. September 27, 2002. Front page and A12. St. Louis, MO.

Humberg, William M. *Open House for Dardenne Presbyterian.* Press Release, Dardenne Presbyterian Church Archives 2002, Dardenne Prairie, MO.

Kirn, Walter. *Lewis and Clark: The Journey That Changed America Forever.* Time Magazine, July 8, 2002. New York, NY, p. 38.

Meyer, Linda. *The Civil War Revisited.* Wentzville Journal, June 2, 2002 Vol. 40, Number 44. Front page.

Missouri Historical Society. Gateway Heritage, *Daniel Boone: Trailblazer to a Nation.* Spring, 1985. p. 28. St. Louis, MO.

Missouri Department of Natural Resources. *First Missouri State Capitol State Historic Site.* Jefferson City, MO.

Missouri's Great River Road. St. Charles. p. 5 Mississippi River Parkway Commission, Missouri Department of Transportation. Jefferson City, MO, undated.

St. Louis, Post Dispatch. *Old Church Revived,* July 9, 1962.p. *[illegible]*—Dardenne Presbyterian Church Archives, Dardenne Prairie, MO.

St. Louis Post-Dispatch. *New Day for Old Dardenne.* Photograph by Reynold Ferguson. St. Louis Post Dispatch. St. Louis, MO, December 11, 1970. General History Archives of Dardenne Presbyterian Church. Dardenne Prairie, MO.

The Daily Banner News. *Dardenne Presbyterian to Mark 150th Anniversary.* November 20, 1968.

The Wentzville Union. *Presbyterian Official to Speak on Anniversary of Dardenne Church.* Wentzville, MO, November 20, 1968.

Yahn, Lillian. *At Dardenne Presbyterian-Dardenne Bible School Scenes-Ladies of the Bible School.* Photos and Story: Lillian Yahn. St. Charles Journal. June 24, 1971. p. 28A. General History Archives of Dardenne Presbyterian Church. Dardenne Prairie, MO.

Booklets and Newsletters

Brazeau Presbyterian Church. *Brazeau Presbyterian Church 175th Anniversary.* Brazeau; Brazeau Presbyterian Church, 1987.

Brown, Daniel T., Ph.D. *The Howell Family Odyssey.* Insights: Francis Howell District Newsletter. Vol. 3 Issue 2. December 1995. St. Charles County, MO.

Brown, Daniel T., Ph.D. *Howell's Prairie.* Francis Howell District Newsletter. June 2000. Vol.7 Issue 3. An excerpt from "Small Glories", St. Charles County, MO.

College Avenue Presbyterian Church. College Ave Presbyterian Church: Elijah P. Lovejoy. Alton: College Avenue Presbyterian Church, 1987.

Dardenne Presbyterian Church. *Dardennaires, 1967-1975* Dardenne Presbyterian Church Archives. Dardenne Prairie: 1975.

Dardenne Presbyterian Church. *Where Do I Fit In?* Dardenne Prairie: Dardenne Presbyterian Church, 2000.

Dardenne Presbyterian Church. *Questions & Answers about "middle way" Presbyterians.* Dardenne Prairie: Dardenne Presbyterian Church, 2000

Dardenne Presbyterian Church. *Observance of the One Hundred Twenty-fifth Anniversary.* Dardenne Prairie: Dardenne Presbyterian Church, 1944.

Dardenne Presbyterian Church. *Dardenne Presbyterian Church.* Cleveland; Presbyterian Publishing House, 1987.

Humberg, William M. *The Lloyd Daugherty Memorial Organ*, 1997, Dardenne Presbyterian Church, Dardenne Prairie, MO.

Poindexter, Mark. St. Charles County Heritage, Vol. 20. No. 4 October 2002 *A Right Smart Little Town, An Anecdotal History of St. Charles*, St. Charles History V, pp. 125-131. St. Charles County Historical Society, St. Charles, MO.

Watson, Sally A. *Dardenne Presbyterian Church.* Dardenne Prairie; Dardenne Presbyterian Church, 1971.

Correspondence

Barbee, Kent Correspondence to Hu Weikart, Chair-Dardenne Presbyterian History Task Force. August 25, 2001.

Boeckman, Laurel. Correspondence to Rev. James W. Williams, Troy Presbyterian Church, Troy, MO, May 3, 1988. General History Archives, Dardenne Presbyterian Church, Dardenne, MO.

Davis, Connie. Correspondence to Diane Rodrique, Dardenne Prairie, MO, March 2002.

Gillette, Gerald W. Correspondence to Rev. Thomas L. Sale, February 27, 1984. Philadelphia, PA.

Loechner, Karen. Correspondence to Diane Rodrique, Dardenne Prairie, MO, March 17, 2002.

Melton, J. Bruce, D.D. Correspondence to Diane Rodrique, March 24, 2002.

Morgan, Harold and Dorothy Correspondence to Diane Rodrique, St. Charles, MO, March, 2002.

Pritchard, Claude H. Presbyterian Church USA, Board of Church Extension, Atlanta, GA, March 19, 1965 to Rev. Stuart H. Salmon, D.D.

Pritchard, Claude Letter to Rev. Stuart H. Salmon, D.D. March 19, 1965. Atlanta, GA.

Pritchard, Claude. Letter to Gene R. Barnard. March 19, 1965. Atlanta, GA.

Pritchard, Claude H. PCUSA, Board of Church Extension, Atlanta, GA, March 19, 1965, to Gene R. Barnard

Salmon, Rev. Stuart H. D.D. Correspondence to Rev. Billy Graham. Overland, MO, December 20, 1962.

Salmon, Rev. Stuart H., D.D. Correspondence to Ira L. Nathan. Overland, MO, October 15, 1963.

Weikart, Hu. Correspondence to Diane Rodrique. Lake St. Louis, MO, March 17, 2002. Dardenne Presbyterian Organ Project. 1996-1998

Sullivan, Brian A. Curatorial Assistant Harvard University Archives. Boston, MA. Correspondence to Rev. Thomas L. Sale, Nov.2, 1995. Archival records, UA III, 5.5.2, vol. IX, 1814-1822.

Miscellaneous

1852 State Census, St. Charles County, MO Dardenne Township, Lineage Press, Bridgeton, MO, 1985.

Apportionments for Benevolences for 1918 and 1919. Dardenne Presbyterian Church Archives.

Dardenne Presbyterian Church History Task Force. *Civil War—Dardenne Presbyterian Church 175th Anniversary Celebration.* Dardenne Prairie, MO, 1994.

Elzea, Jane. *History of Dardenne Presbyterian Church.* undated.

Giddings-Lovejoy Presbytery Board Records. p. 41, April 1830. Photocopies.

Illustrated Atlas Map of St. Charles County, MO W.R. Brink & Co. of Illinois. 1875

McPheeters, Harold L. *The McPheeters Family.* Atlanta, GA, 1995. Dardenne Presbyterian History Archives, Dardenne Prairie, MO.

Melton, Dr. J. Bruce. *An Organ Transplant or The Body of Christ Gets a New Musical Heart.* undated, St. Charles, MO.

*Minutes of the Missouri Presbytery, 1817-1869.*Dardenne Presbyterian Church Archives. Photocopies courtesy of the Presbyterian Historical Society at Philadelphia, PA.

Missouri Presbytery Records. *Organization of Churches, April 20, 1819.* Dardenne Presbyterian Church Archives.

Orf, Bernice and Rose. *History of The Orf Farm-1880-1995*. St. Charles County, MO, May 1996.

Stephen Ministries, *Stephen Series brochure*, St. Louis, MO, undated

Stewart, Helen *History of Dardenne Presbyterian Church*, Dardenne Prairie, MO, March 1970.

Sullivan, Brian A. (Divinity School) *General Catalogue of the Theological Seminary, Andover, Massachusetts 1808-1908*. Thomas Todd, Printer. Boston, Mass. Harvard College Library Jan. 30, 1939.

Watson Hall Information Files. 1970. Dardenne Presbyterian Archives, Dardenne Presbyterian Church. Dardenne Prairie, MO.

Wilson, Mrs. William C. *History of Dardenne Presbyterian Church*, Dardenne Prairie, MO, Sept. 1944.

Appendix A

The Dedicated Leaders of Dardenne
Presbyterian Church

During its 185-year history, Dardenne Presbyterian has been blessed with dedicated men and women who have, in their own way, made significant contributions to the church. From our founding minister, Rev. Charles S. Robinson, to our current pastors, Rev. Gary Myers and Rev. Lew Kimmel, we are indebted to the men who have given so generously of their time and talent to serve God and provide for the spiritual needs of Dardenne members. All information is provided courtesy of the Dardenne Presbyterian Church Registry.

Throughout this book two phrases regularly appear in connection with the ministers who serve or have served our church. A **Stated Supply Minister** is an ordained minister appointed by the Presbytery to serve the congregation when an installed minister is not available. An **Installed Minister** an ordained minister who is called by the church to serve its congregation. The Presbytery installs the minister. The minister then provides leadership to his (or her) congregation until retirement, illness or death ends his/her service. When the current installed pastor is no longer able to serve, the congregation issues a call for a new minister.

DATES	NAME	TITLE
1819-1827	Rev. Charles S. Robinson	Founding Minister
1827-1830	Rev. William S. Lacy	Stated Supply Pastor
1830-1831	Rev. John M. Ball	Stated Supply Pastor
1831-1833	Rev. Samuel Finley	Stated Supply Pastor
1832	*Rev. Douglas	Stated Supply Pastor
1834-1835	Rev. Warren Nichols	Stated Supply Pastor
1835-1840	Rev. Hiram Chamberlain	Stated Supply Pastor
1839	*Rev. Matthews	Stated Supply Pastor
1840-1844	Rev. Robert G. Barrett	Stated Supply Pastor
1842-1844	Rev. Hiram Chamberlain	Stated Supply Pastor
1844	Rev. Chamberlain, Rev. Harleigh Blackwell & Rev. William S. Potts	Moderators of Session
4/12/1844-10/6/1844	Thomas Watson	Licentiate of Presbytery
11/10/1844-4/15/1888	Thomas Watson	1st Installed Pastor d. 6/2/1888

DATES	NAME	TITLE
1868-1878	Adam Lamb	Professor/Teacher
6-11/1888	Revs. T.C. Smith & Rev. R.G. Barrett	Stated Supply Pastors
12/1888-11/4/1892	Rev. Samuel McCluer Watson	Stated Supply Pastor
11/4/1892- 4/9/1925	**Rev. Samuel McCluer Watson**	**2nd Installed Pastor** d. 4/9/1925
1925-1929	Dr. William C. Colby	Stated Supply Pastor
1929-1941	*Rev. Daryl Davis, Dr. William Crowe, Rev. Fred Reeves, Rev. Glen Williams, Rev. Herbert Watson, Dr. Walter Langtry	Guest Pastors
	Rev. Mac Crowe	Student Pastor
1941-1943	Rev. L.V. MacPherson	Stated Supply Pastor
1944-1945	** Dr. Herbert Watson	Stated Supply Pastor
1946	Rev. L.A. McCutcheon	Stated Supply Pastor
1947-1949	Rev. Charles E. Morton	Stated Supply Pastor
1949-1952	Rev. N.C. Griffith	Stated Supply Pastor
1953-1956	Charles Ruffner Watson	Lay Pastor
1956-1957	Dr. Herbert Watson	Stated Supply Pastor
1957-1967	Dr. Stuart S. Salmon	Stated Supply Pastor
1966 (3 mos. summer)	Mr. Nick Fenger	Student Pastor
9/1966-5/1967	Dr. Herbert Watson	Stated Supply Pastor
5/1/1967-10/4/1970	Mr. Charles M. Bunce	Lay Leader
5/1/1967-10/4/1967	Rev. James Duncan (Troy, MO)	Moderator for Lay Pastor
10/4/1970-6/26/1973	**Rev. Charles M. Bunce**	**3rd Installed Pastor** d. 6/26/1973
6/2/1974-12/31/1997	**Rev. Thomas L. Sale**	**4th Installed Pastor** retired: 12/31/1997
	Rev. James Sibley	Associate Pastor
1978-1980	Rev. Robert J. Alwood	Associate Pastor
1982-1989	Rev. Michael W. Jackson	Associate Pastor
1989-1991	Rev. Paul Coats	Associate Pastor
1994-1996	Dr. Robert Falconer	Parish Associate
9/1996-12/31/1997	Rev. Gary Myers	1st Co-Pastor
1/1/1998-Present	**Rev. Gary Myers**	**5th Installed Pastor**
8/1998-Present	Rev. Lewis. Kimmel	Associate Pastor

* Occasional guest ministers.

** Dr. Herbert Watson served Dardenne three different times: 1944–1945, 1956–1957, 1966–1967

In addition to being blessed with dedicated pastors, the congregation consists of generous people who are willing to share their time and talent with others. Among them are the Elders who serve on the Session—the governing body of the church, Deacons, Trustees and Stephen Ministers, who although involved with other projects in the church, willingly and joyfully accept additional leadership responsibility.

Elders oversee the general operations of the church through various committees. Deacons see to the service of the people and the community. The Trust Board conducts the civil business of the church. Stephen Ministers support the pastors by counseling and assisting members of the congregation.

The Session

The Elders	The Diaconate
2004	**2004**
Barbara Busse, Rob Goodrich, Larry Mundhenk, Alice Ross, Debbie Schuck, Hu Weikart, Brittany Kohl (Youth Rep)	Marvin Cave, Carryl Grubbs, Stuart Huddleston, Gary Nassau, Dennis Stewart, Lisa Mundhenk (Youth Rep.)
2005	**2005**
Jack Grubbs, Joel Heidbreder, Rik Johnson, Vicky McCoy, Mike Merritt, Rick Sabbert	Pat Boulch, Robin Brothers, Tim Mobarak, Ray Schraymeyer, Bob Underwood
2006	**2006**
Dick Buchanan, Joan Grossmann, Art McCluer, Jackie McCracken, Barbara Stiles, Chip Wright, Judy Lowery—Clerk of the Session	Vince Gehrin, Nick Giannakis, Karen Kraemer, Martha Orf, Jim Pratt

The Trustees receive, hold, manage and transfer property, both real and personal, and accept and execute deeds of title for the church. Their purpose being is to manage special funds for the church.

The Trustees

<u>2004</u>	<u>2005</u>	<u>2006</u>
Dave Schlansker	Steve Brown	Joy Brown
Bob Whipple	Jim Mouser	Clyde Mouser

The Stephen Ministers

A rapidly growing program, the Stephen Ministry is a group of trained volunteers who are asked to dedicate at least two years of service to the lay ministry and assist the pastors with counseling and problem solving for members of the congregation. As of June of 2004, the Dardenne Presbyterian Stephen Ministry consisted of:

Leaders

Pastor Lew Kimmel   **Dorothy Morgan**   **David Brothers**   **Margie Conrad**
Bill Fader

Stephen Ministers

Lois Bennett	Shirley Barnes	Carol Bell-Clark	Nancy Fanter
Becky Flowers	Jennifer Kessler	Ralph Kessler	Doris Liesman
Marlene Meier	Joan McClean	Cathy McCulloch	Hugh McCulloch
Doug Paramore	Sonja Paramore	Marjorie Pettig	Charlene Smith
Marilyn Smith	Tom Soell	Barb Wyatt	

0-595-32638-2

Printed in the United States
21184LVS00003B/211-270